The Tamil Alphabet and Its Mystic Aspect

The Tamil Alphabet and Its Mystic Aspect

P. V. MANICKAM NAICKER

GYAN

Published by

Gyan Publishing House
5, Ansari Road
Daryaganj, New Delhi-110002
Phone: 011-47034999, 9811692060
E-mail: books@gyanbooks.com

Distribution Network
gyanbooks.com
India, USA, Canada, UK, Australia, France

ISBN : 978-81-212-4083-3 (PB)
First Published, 1917

2nd Impression 2020

Printed at: Gyan Press, Delhi.

The Tamil Alphabet and Its Mystic Aspect
Author: P. V. Manickam Naicker

INTRODUCTION.

I have much pleasure in writing this introduction to the paper read by Mr. Manickam Naicker at the last session of the South Indian Association at which I presided. Portions only of the paper, giving a succinct outline of the subject, were then read out, but the whole paper is now published.

His demonstration of the transformation of the letter ஓ into அ and of the letter அ into the other letters of the alphabet his production of the Mantric forms from the letter அ symbolising their legends, his exposition of the coincidences of natural forms with the Pranava letter ஓ, and his quotations illustrating the mystic-philosophy under-lying the Tamil forms and language seem to be original discoveries and are very interesting and instructive.

As I don't believe in the theory of "mere curious coincidences" especially when they become numerous, I think that the balance of probability leans very much in favour of the main theory of the lecturer. It is therefore very probable that the letters of the Tamil alphabet were devised by a great Rishi on a definite philosophical plan. As a rule no new suggestion or discovery is accepted by the people without hesitation and so the author himself does not demand abrupt acceptance of his principles. Especially in the matter of details, there is room for great divergence of opinion and the author evidently keeps an open mind, showing that though he is "possessed" of new and startling ideas, he also "possesses" them and is not their slave. The subject, however, is one of such absorbing interest that even a gentleman of such wide reading and culture as the author (the author's deep knowledge of embryology, geology, archaelogy, and other subjects showing that he is not a mere lop-sided and narrow-minded scholar) might be led into minor errors unless other scholars assist him with free criticisms and suggestions which he invites so modestly in his "Address to those concerned". I believe that beyond intellect is Intuition and that Intuitional Inspiration comes to those (Darwin and Newton being great examples) who have got a passion for Truth without being swayed by prejudice and conceit and have thought and studied long with that passion in their heart. I may be permitted to express my opinion (for whatever it is worth) that the author seems to have had intuitional glimpses of some universal mystic Truths in consequence of such deep study and meditation.

The author does not profess to be a deep Sanscrit scholar. I have no doubt that very clever critics are sure to fasten on a few errors and a few weak arguments which may be found here and there and try to cast ridicule in a wholesale manner on the author on that account. That is an ordeal which all authors who put forward works of intuitional originality (especially where the works contain mystic Truths) ought to be prepared to pass through. Fortunately, they mostly not only survive the ordeal but become better and purer for the ordeal. Our author is, I believe, prepared to suffer in such "good company" and will (I have little doubt) survive similarly. I believe that every later edition of the author's work would get rid of the weak points in the earlier editions and demonstrate by further illustrations drawn from the wide circle of scientific and mystic lore the strength of the foundation-verities on which the work is based. If no later edition is called for, it must be due to the root-ideas being too "futuristic" but seeing that the humanworld is moving very fast in these days I do not myself believe that the work has been too prematurely born.

The subject matter dealt with by the author is such that it was necessary for him to make brief but specific mention of his views about (1) the Tamil phonetic, (2) the importance of Tholkappium to the historians, (3) the status and age of Tamil. (4) the Aryan migration theories, (5) the South Indian rules of life, (6) the Vatteluthu character of the Tamil language and a few other minor subjects. In all these, he has clearly, though briefly, expressed his views which are also original and interesting. It is earnestly hoped that his papers on these subjects would also soon be published.

The Tamil phonetics were all along considered to be defective but Mr. Naicker says that there is no other more perfect phonetic system than that of Tamil and that he demonstrated the same in the Wesley College Hall. His theory of one migration of the Aryans from South India (whether it was the *primeordeal* migration or not may not be quite so certain) and the later migration from Central Asia to the west and south, as supported by some apparently strong scientific grounds, deserves consideration. His theory about the origin and the extinction of the Vatteluthu characters synchronising with the period of the Pallava influence, is equally interesting and seems probable. His remonstrance against certain modern Brahmin authors and his strong argument to show that the South Indian Brahmins are by blood high class Tamils, far from indicating any estrangement in him, show clearly that he really admires and loves them and likes to own them and to be owned by them as his kith and kin as he expressly avows. However, he naturally and rightly does not relish the irreverential reference to Thiruvalluvar's great work by one of the said authors.

One would see that if even a tithe of Mr. Naicker's views on the Tamil language is correct, (and I for one believe that many of the root ideas are coriect) he places the Tamil language on a very high pedestal. When such an enthusiast is available, all lovers of the language and the people will do well to co-operate so that he may bring out his other researches as well, which are sure to be equally interesting and useful. One of his original works *viz.*, 'Calculograph,' a new method in Mathematics covering the whole range of the theoretical Mathematics, has been very eulogistically recognised by English authorities and I am informed that the Secretary of State too has sanctioned his deputation to England to complete that research, and hence we can place reliance on his competency for original work.

Mr. Naicker's time now being available for use in his own country, he will do yeomen service by publishing his other researches pertaining to South Indians and their language and their antiquarian eminence. I would further strongly recommend his publishing the researches in Tamil as well, as they are sure to have an ennobling influence on the people of our country.

Invoking the blessings of my Lord Govinda on the author's life and activities I have much pleasure to introduce his present subject to the public who ought to feel obliged to the author for his labours.

1—5—1917. T. SADASIVA IYER.

HON'BLE MR. PRESIDENT AND GENTLEMEN,

The subject I wish to present to you this evening is "The Tamil Alphabet and its Mystic aspect."

The presentation of any mystic subject in this matter-of-fact materialistic times needs necessarily an explanation and apology. However much you were delighted in the subject of the previous lecture, you must be physically tired of sitting, and so I do not wish to detain you long. I shall, therefore, with your permission, drop the explanation and apology, and go straight into the subject.

Transformation of letters producing strange Coincidences with the Hindu Mystics.

It is a noteworthy fact that, out of all the letters of the Tamil alphabet, the முளை யெழுத்து or the Pranava letter ஒ—the short O—is one which has evaded the skill, ingenuity and labours of the evolutionists and obliged the archeologists and epigraphists to admit that they do not know as yet its evolution, as it retains a constant form from the earliest of the known inscriptions down to the present. The form of some of the other letters will be disputed by the epigraphists. I shall revert to this point later on if time permits.

First of all, I shall give you some amusing, if not interesting, kindergarten demonstration of the kaleidoscopic transformation of the முளை யெழுத்து, that **constant** ஒ, producing primarily the letter அ and secondarily other letters of the alphabet and the Moola Manthras—the basic holy symbols or letters—and discuss their philosophic significance in due course.

Figure 1 shows the natural form of the letter ஒ (short O) in firm lines. The structure of this letter comprises one main curve A B N resembling the outline of an embryo with N as the navel point, a slanting down stroke N C occupying a position analogous to that of the umbilical cord and a cross stroke D C E occupying the position of the placenta. If the slanting and cross strokes N-C D E are bodily turned round 180 degrees about the navel point N as a pivot, so that they may occupy the position shown in dotted lines N C_1 D_1 E $_1$, the resulting figure is the Tamil letter அ—the short A. It will thus be seen that the component parts of the two letters ஒ and அ are the same, but only the slanting and the cross strokes occupy two opposite positions.

Figure 2 shows the Tamil letter அ—short A—in three segments marked A, U, M. The segments are made distinct by allowing narrow blank spaces between them. The same three segments are rearranged below producing the letter ஒ (short O.) The long stroke marked A is placed over the letter ஒ. With the head stroke, the letter is short O, whereas without the stroke it will be long O, according to the recognised Tamil grammars from the ancient Tholkappium down to Nannul. The rules or Sutras of the Tholkappium regarding the dots are :—"மெய்யினியல்பு புள்ளியொடு நிலையல்," i.e., the nature of the mute consonant is to *rest* with a dot ; and "எகர ஒகரத்தியற் கையு மற்றே", i. e., the nature of the letters short எ and short ஒ is the same as above. The Nannul Sutra regarding the same is :—" தொல்லைவடிவின வெல்லா வெழுத்துமாண் டெய்து மெகர மொகர

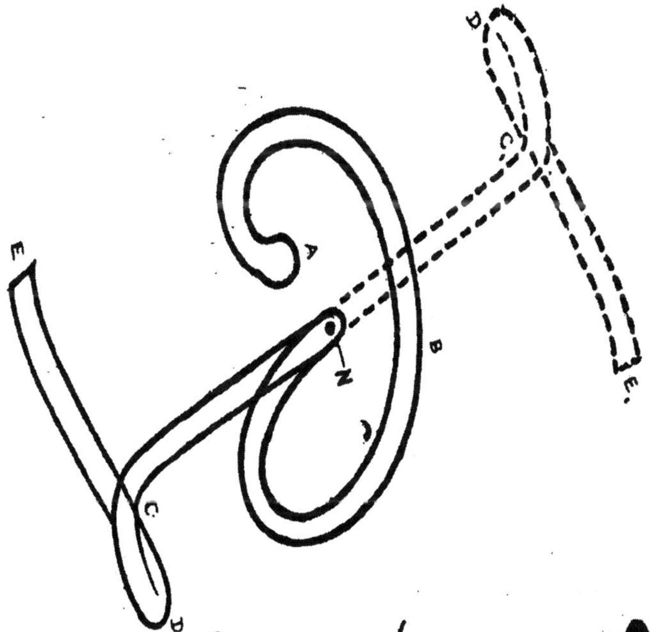

Fig. 1.

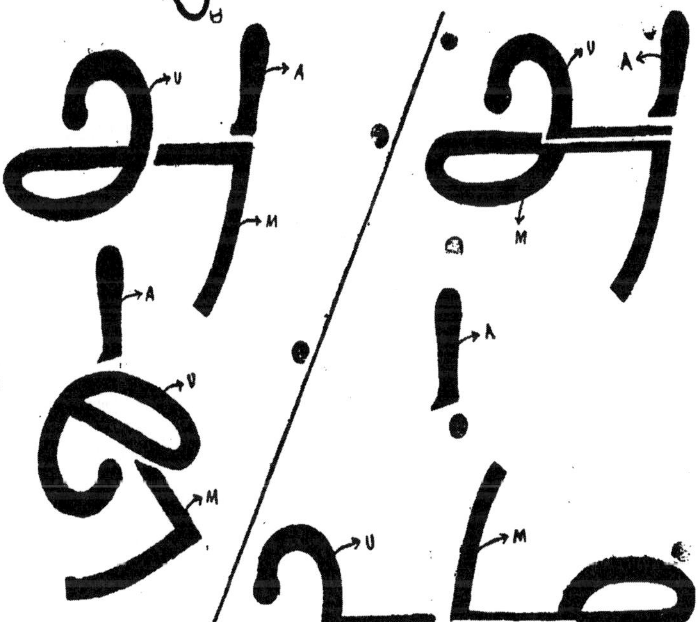

Fig. 2.

Fig. 3.

மெய்ப்புள்ளி," i. e., all letters have the same forms as of yore and of them the letters short எ and short ஒ have dots similar to mute consonants.

The dot now in use is the round one and the question arises whether the dot referred to in the Tamil grammars is the round dot, as at present or the long stroke or both. The Tamil word used to denote 'dot' is " புள்ளி " (Pulli). If the root meaning of this word " புள்ளி " is ascertained, it will be seen that it means "that which is like புள்". The root " புள் " means either a bird in general or a short piece of stick used as a playing instrument by boys. This short stick is similar in shape to the long stroke. In play, it is laid over a fulcrum and one end of it is struck with a long stick. The short stick "புள்" flies off as a bird and this may be the reason why the word " புள் " means both 'a bird in general' and 'a short stick used for play.'. The word புள்ளி means also a round point. Therefore the question reduces to where the round dot, and where the long stroke should be used.

The form of the dot seen in the older Tamil inscriptions known is the long stroke with a broad head and a tapering bottom. I may refer for instance to the early 9th century inscriptions of Nandivikramavarman. However, the dot disappeared altogether in the later inscriptions for nearly 8 centuries and reappeared as round points in modern times. The proper form of the consonant-dot recognised by the ancients seems, therefore, to be the long stroke similar to the form of a Linga. The system of the transformation of letters, as is being demonstrated to you this evening, also gives invariably the long stroke of the Linga form for the consonant-dot, wherever it occurs. I have so far shown the mutual transformation of ஓ into அ and அ into ஓ.

Figure 3, page 3 shows the Tamil letter அ in three different segments. To render them distinct, they are separated by narrow blank spaces. The three segments, when rearranged, form the Linga and the word உம meaning Parvathi. It will be noticed that the letter அ is a monogram comprising the letters அ, உ and ம. The whole figure is அ, the top portion is உ and the bottom portion is ம placed upside down. As these three letters அ, உ and ம are the very three elements of the மூன் றெழுத்து or Pranava ஓ, the letter அ comprises the Pranavaic elements fully and seems to signifiy the principles of Trinity in Unity and Unity in Trinity. The word உ ம itself taken out of the letter அ, if divided into its component parts, the three letters உ, ம், அ are obtained. Thus in the Pranava ஓ we have அ, உ, ம், whereas in உ ம we get the same three letters in another order viz. உ, ம், அ. The first order ending in the mute consonant ம் seems to signify the resting aspect of Siva, and the second order ending in the letter அ, the active aspect of Sakthi or Parvathi. When the letters உ and ம are separated from the letter அ, there still remains the long stroke in the Linga form, which, if placed over ம, produces the mute consonant ம், signifying that, in the presence of Siva, the letter ம or Maya becomes mute and inactive.

Shastras describe Sakthi and Maya (active power and myth) as a monster with two heads and one body thus emphasising their inseparable character.

The above idea seems to be well signified by the arrangement of the two letters உ and ம in the letter அ having two

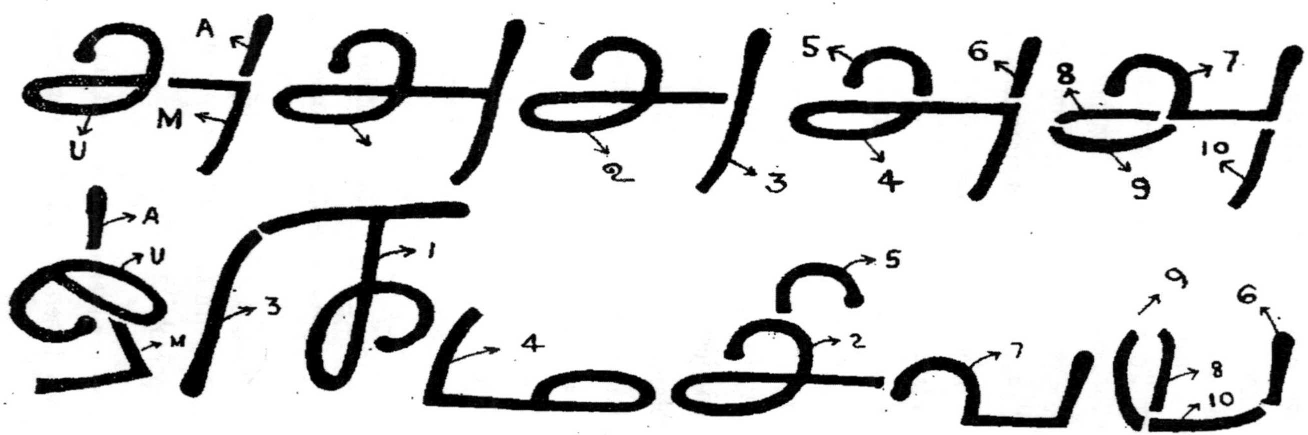

8

separate heads and one body, Fig. 3 page. 3. If these two letters உ and ம should be separated the stem or body has to be rent asunder longitudinally See. Fig.

The immutability, the indestructability, self existence, oneness and all other attributes of the Lord or 'பதி' are well signified by the long stroke, the Linga form, remaining apart and intact in all the transformations under demonstration. In all the formations, this long stroke attaches itself by its leg only to produce other letters. This is not the case with the other parts of the letter அ.

Page 6 shows 5 letters அ divided into various segments. The first letter has three segments marked A, U, M, the next letter is in one piece, marked 1, the next is in two segments marked 2 and 3, the next is in three segments marked 4, 5, and 6, and the last letter is in four segments marked 7, 8, 9, and 10. All these segments are rearranged to form the Moola Manthra "ஓநமசிவய" The three segments, A, U, M, of the first letter அ form the letter ஓ in the Manthra. The ten segments of the remaining letters அ form the five letters "நமசிவய" of the Panchakshara or ஐந்தெழுத்து. The coincidence of the number of letters viz. 5 in "நமசிவய" with the number of faces of Siva, and the ten component segments of these five letters with the number of hands of Siva, is worthy of note. In rearranging the segments of the five letters அ, we have obtained the five letters of the Panchakshara "நமசிவய", and yet the Pranava letter ஓ comes out extra signifying the immutability of Eswara, though the five letters "நமசிவய" come out to perform the Panchakrithya or the five acts of Siva viz. Srishti, Thithi, Sankara, Throbava,

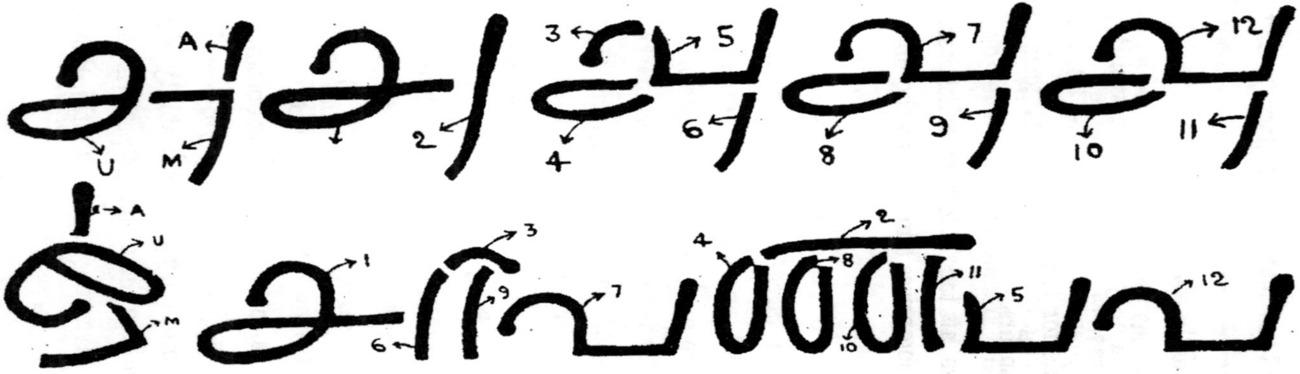

and Anugraha. The philosophic value of each letter of the Panchakshara "நமசிவய" can be most distinctly and accurately read in the forms of the various segments which go to produce each letter, taking out their value from their position in the original Moola Pranava ஓ or அ. This will lead to a lengthy discourse unsuitable for this occasion, and so I pass over to another Moola Manthra.

Page 8 shows at top 5 letters அ in various segments. The first letter அ comprises three segments marked A. U. M., and the remaining letters அ comprise 12 segments in all marked 1 to 12. The three segments of the first letter அ are rearranged to form the Pranava or முன்னெழுத்து ஓ. The 12 segments of the remaining letters அ are rearranged to produce the Shatakshara or six letters சரவணபவ. The coincidence of the number of letters in சரவணபவ viz. 6, and the number of segments comprised viz. 12, with the number of faces and hands respectively of the deity, Muruga, signified by the Manthra is worthy of note. Here too, as in the case of Panchakshara, the Pranava முன்னெழுத்து ஓ representing Eswara remains extra, signifying the immutability of Eswara. The philosophic value of each letter of the Manthra can be read from the forms of the segments, and how the permutation of the letters convey the ideas of Ashtakrya or the eight functions can also be clearly seen from the forms.

It is also worthy of note that the origin of the two Manthras, Panchakshara and Shatakshara, is the same 5 letters அ signifying that the two deities Siva and Muruga are the two different Moorthas or forms of the same original Eswara as stated in Shastras. This sort of identification of Muruga

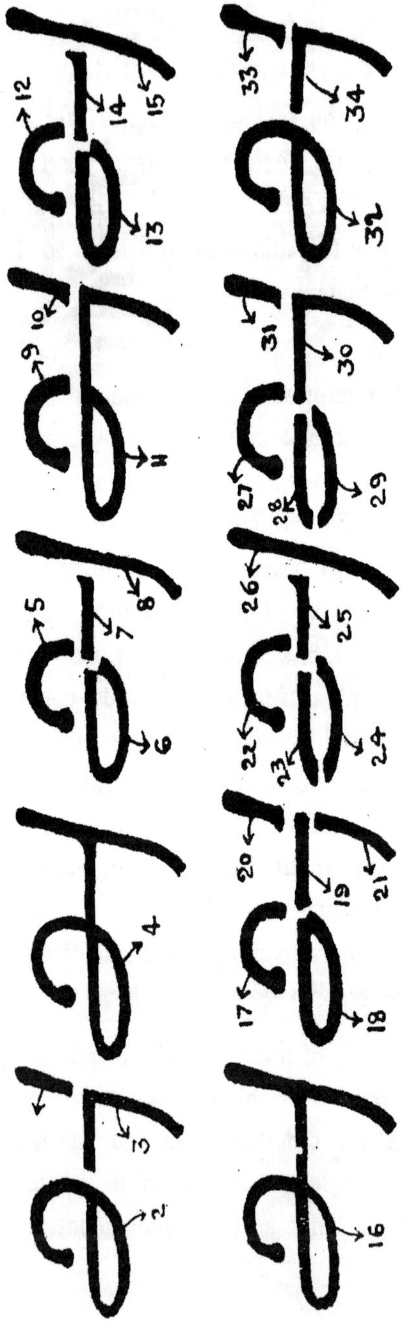

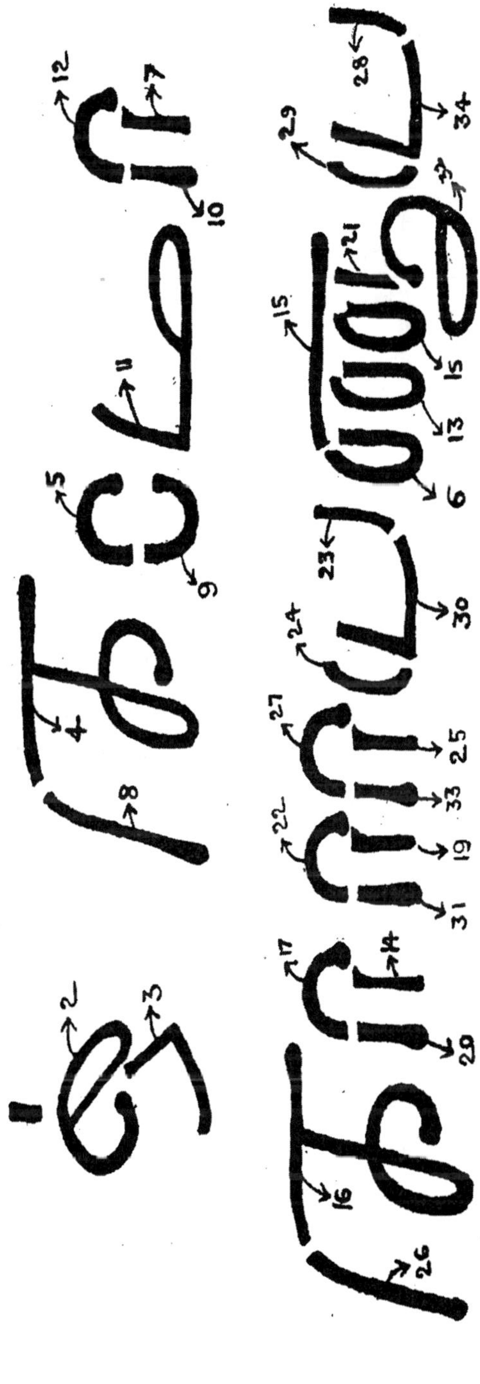
2
3
4
8
5
9
11
12
7
10
17
22
27
24
23
15
29
28
16
26
14
21
20
31
19
33
25
30
6
13
15
32
34

with Siva from the 5 Moola Pranavas அ is nothing novel. As pointed out by the Gnaniar Swamigal of Thirupapuliyur, the Shastras themselves identify them as one and the same by totalling the number of faces, hands and eyes of each; five faces, ten hands and fifteen eyes of Siva make 30 ; and the six faces, twelve hands and twelve eyes of Muruga also make 30. In Siva the eyes are numerous, whereas in Muruga the hands are numerous, signifying that the Muruga Manthra, Shatakshara, is more suited for Ashtakryas than the Siva Manthra.

Page 10 shows ten Pranava letters அ in various segments numbering in all 34. These 34 segments are rearranged in page 11 to form the complicated Ashtakshara or எட்டெழுத்து Moola-manthra "ஓ நமோ நாராயணாய." Here the Pranava letter ஓ does not stand extra, but counts as one of the eight letters and the total number of segments also include the 3 segments of ஓ. Even in this very complicated form of the Ashtakshara, there is perfect method and system in the transformation of the letters. The number of Pranava letters அ coincides with the number of Avathars or incarnations of Vishnu *viz.* ten, which in turn comprise 5 Deva Avathars or incarnations without the medium of womb, and 5 human Avathars or incarnations with the medium of womb. One school of Hindu theology would say that these ten Avathars or incarnations correspond to the ten faces of the deity Parâparâ, the united body of Parâ and Parai, each having five faces; the Para's five faces giving rise to the 5 Deva Avathars, and the Parai's 5 faces giving rise to the 5 human Avatharas.

The number of segments viz. 34 of the ten Moola Pranava letters அ producing the Ashtakchara coincides with the number of hands of the 10 incarnations. The five Deva Avathars, viz. Macha (fish), Koorma (Tortoise), Varâha (pig), Karki (horse), and Narasimha (the man-lion) had four hands each making twenty in all. Out of the human Avathars or incarnations, Rama, Parasurama, and Balarama, as one Vishnavite school would reckon, or Rama, Parasurama and Budha as another school would count, had only two hands each making 6 in all. Vâmanâ had two hands at birth, but when he cast off his human form and appeared in his Visvarupa or immeasurable figure, he put forth four hands (Bâghavatha Purana.) Krishna, though born out of a womb, had four hands at birth, but retracted two of them immediately afterwards, according to the same Purana. Thus, these two incarnations had 8 hands in all. Now, collecting all the hands of the ten incarnations, we have 34. This coincidence of the indisputably lengthy arithmetical calculation of the hands of the incarnations, and the segments of the ten letters அ which produce the Ashtakshara or the holy eight letters, is very very strange indeed. It is not my present theme either to consider or to say whether the legends pertaining to the various deities of the Indian pantheon were constructed from the forms and conditions of the letters or that the letters were constructed in a manner to signify the legends.

Now, the abstruse statement in our Shastras that all the Moola Manthras are only the development of the Panchakshara, and that the Panchakshara itself is the development of the Moola Pranava or மூல வெழுத்து ௐ, may be verified in the forms. That all the Manthras evolve out of the Pranava ௐ is borne out by the fact that the letter ௐ is transformable into அ by merely rotating the stem about its navel end, and that all the Manthras evolve out of the letter அ which is ஓ in another form. That all the Maha Manthras are only Panchaksharas may be verified in three different ways. First of all, the Panchakshara "ஓ-நமசிவய", is produced from five Pranava letters அ. The Shatakchara "ஓ சரவணபவ" is also produced from the same five Pranava letters அ. The Ashtakshara "ஓ-நமோ நாராயணய" is produced from twice five Pranava letters அ. Next, the Ashtakshara comprises two main and distinct parts *viz.*, "ஓ நமோ" and "நாராயணய." It is clear that the latter is Panchakshara, or five letters, and it further commences in "ந" and ends in "ய" as in 'நமசிவய.' The first part "ஓ நமோ" contains only three letters, but, if the first letter ஓ is expanded into its elements அ, உ, ம், we get five letters in the first part also. The third and more interesting verification is by deleting the repeating letters from the Manthras. The Pranava or முதெழுத்து, ஓ, is common to all the three Manthras. Out of the remaining letters in the Panchakshara, there is no repetition of any letter. The Shatakshara "சரவணபவ" repeats one letter வ, and, if the duplicate வ is expunged the number of letters left in the Shatakshara is only five. The Ashtakshara after omitting ஓ consists of only seven letters "நமோ நாராயணய," in which the two letters ந and ய repeat. If the duplicate letters ந and ய are expunged from the Manthra, the remainder is only five.

It now remains to examine page 15, in which two sets having each four letters அ are shown. These sets have 10 and 13 segments producing in the rearrangement the two words "அரி சுவடி" and "நால் மறை," respectively. These two words, out of all words in the language have special import which will

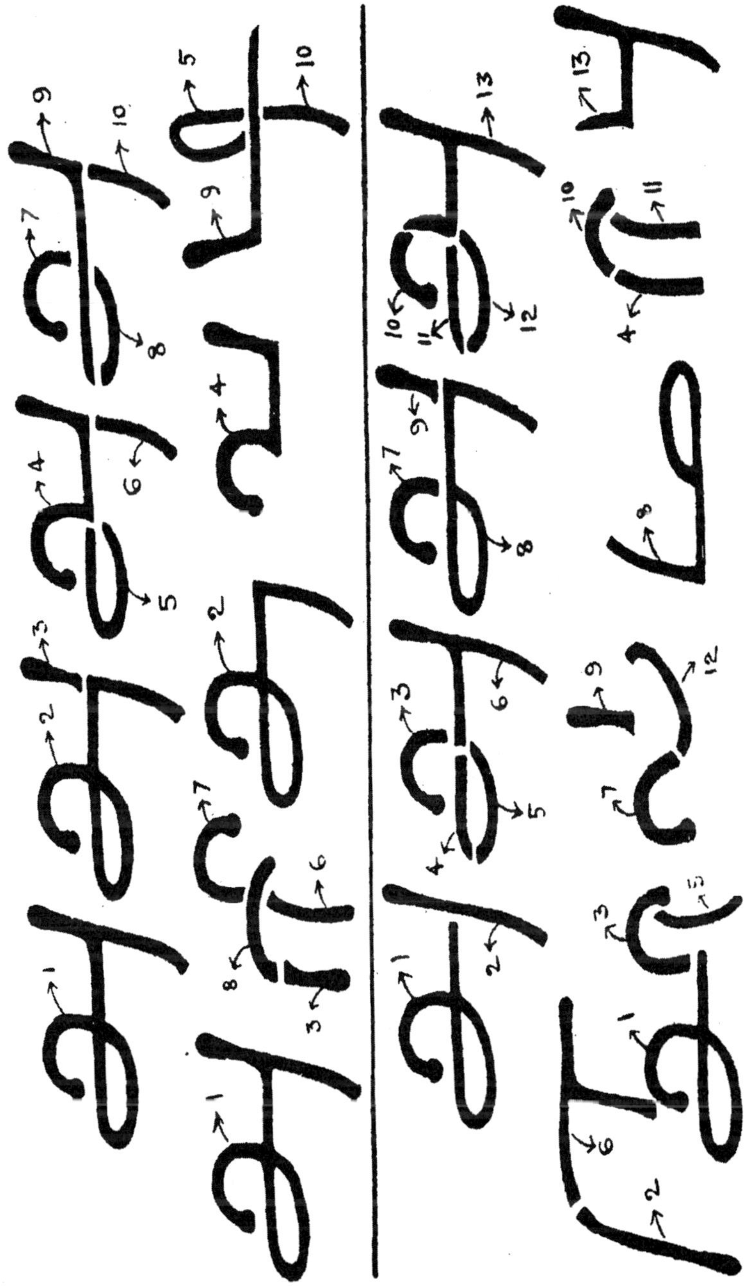

be dealt with later on. It is enough here to point out that these two words are formed of five letters each as in Panchakshara. Four Pranava letters அ produce, in turn, the two different words "அரி சுவடி." and "நால் மரபு." The Vedas are supposed to have been produced by four Pranavas. Now I wish to invite your attention to the coincidence of the legend as to the origin of Vedas from four Pranavas with the transformation of four letters Pranava producing the abovesaid two words. The subject dealt with in "அரி சுவடி" and in the chapter "நால் மரபு" in Tholkappium is nothing but the Tamil alphabet in four significant classes *viz.* "உயிரெழுத்து" vowels or Jeevathma letters, "மெய்யெழுத்து" consonants or Maya letters, "உயிர் மெய்யெழுத்து" syllabic consonants or letters of Jeevathma in Maya and "தனிநிலை" or "ஆய்தம்" meaning the one immutable letter. It will be necessary to revert to this in some more detail later on.

The demonstration of the kaleidoscopic transformation of the Pranava letter or மூலவெழுத்து ஓ producing the various Moola Manthras and the two words last mentioned may be closed with a summary of the most salient points.

The letter ஓ is transformable into அ by merely rotating the stem through 180 degrees. The letters அ used for the demonstration of the transformation of letters are all of one uniform shape and size. The segments cut are invariably the integral parts of the letter அ as the angles and curves of the letter itself would suggest. The Moola Manthras and the two words produced by transformation have letters of noticeably exquisite shape and proportions and uniformity of form and principles of construction. Where letters repeat they are identical in their parts. The number of segments and letters seems to signify the legends pertaining to the Moola Manthras and words. The delineation of the transformed letters signify their mystic value. The Manthras and words dealt with are formed with the minimum number of segments, and all attempts to reduce the number of segments any further prove futile.

In the transformation of the Manthras and the two holy words, all the parts of an integral number of letters அ are used up. Though all the other Tamil words can be constructed in a similar manner out of parts of letters அ, the words which take up all the parts of an integral number of letters அ are extremely few. This statement may be tested by actual experiment.

If these are accidental coincidences, they must be extremely strange coincidences, the like of which is impossible to meet in any other branch of knowledge. In fact, the so-called coincidences so far mentioned, form an infinitesimal part of further coincidences of Shastraic statements, with the significance of the forms of letters, which for want of time and for other reasons cannot be dealt with here *in extenso.*

Enquiry into the Rationale of the Mystic.

With the above prelude, I may now enter into a discourse on the subject proper—"The Tamil Alphabet and its Mystic aspect."

The Tamil language abounds in mystic literature so much that, if all works that have references to mysticism should be set aside, the rest will be nothing except the much advertised Tamil *novelkal* of to-day. Till a few decades ago, there was only one school of thought as regards the origin and use of the language, *viz.*, the Mystic School, which told us that the Tamil language was given by God Siva to Agasthia, who, in turn, prescribed it to the South Indians, and that its use was to *reach* God. Thiruvalluvar emphasises this in his couplets :—

கற்றதனாலாய பய னென்கொல் வாலறிவன்
நற்றாழ் தொழா ரெனின்.

" No fruit have men of all their studied lore
" Save they the 'Purely Wise One's' feet adore." (Pope)

ஒருமைக்கட்டான் கற்ற கல்வி யொருவற்
கெழுமையு மேமாப்புடைத்து.

" The man who store of learning gains
" In one, through seven worlds, bliss attains." (Pope)

நிறை மொழி மாந்தர் பெருமை நிலத்து
மறை மொழி காட்டிவிடும்.

" The might of men whose word is never vain.
" The 'secret word' shall to the earth proclaim. " (Pope)

While this Mystic School, which the present day materialists would style 'the School of Ignorance', prevailed, there was perfect unity of thought in assuming that God gave us the language, probably because ignorance is bliss.

The present school may be called the " Rational School ". It includes the archaeologists, epigraphists, ethnologists, palaeontologists, historians and such like who would not accept anything without a reason, and their *rationale* being necessarily limited to the normal comprehension of the human mind, no credit would be attached to powers of special intuition which the Mystic School would claim. The so-called normal is not a fixed standard for all times and places as powers of comprehension differ between individuals and differs in the same individual. In contrast with the old School of ignorance, the Rational School has the vast diversity of opinion as regards the origin and use of the language. If there are ten branches of investigation in this school, there are ten times ten opinions on the same subject. The Sanskritist endeavours to trace everything to Sanskrit, the Western to the west, the Eastern to the east, the Christian to ancient Babylon, the Hindu to Kurukshetra, and the Tamilian, as this lecturer is, for his part would trace with equal if not greater success, everything to Tamil and South India.

We are certain so far that all of them cannot be wholly correct. It is not impossible that all of them are wrong entirely.

The Mystic School had its absolute sway for ages. Even the very evolutionists' law of the survival of the fittest should indicate, that there must be some substantial foundation in that school to account for its very long life. The foundation cannot be the mere ignorance of the Indian nation. Our ancients, who bequeathed to us perfect astronomy, music, pharmacopaea, philosophy, grammar, prosody and what not, are not likely to have played an altogether idiosyncracic part for ages in their mystic lore.

The Rational School, which claims to supersede the Mystic School, should, in fairness, have first applied their criterion of research to discern what is chaff and what is grain in the mystic lore instead of treating it with wholesale contempt.

To discover the *rationale* of the Mystic was my pursuit for nearly three decades. I cannot say that I have solved it entirely, but I have a lot of data likely to be of use to more competent scholars for further research. The subject is a progressive one just as any branch of mathematics, so that its advanced parts cannot be dealt with, without going through the rudimentary portions, which alone can be placed before this learned audience this evening.

In dealing with the alphabet, both for ordinary and mystic purposes, definite classification into two parts, viz. (1) Phonetics and (2) Form, is necessary. As I wish to produce some slides illustrating the rationality of the forms this evening, I have to pass over the phonetics with only a few remarks. The sounds are or rather the pronounciation is, of the Tamil alphabet minutely and scientifically defined in all the available Tamil Grammars, from the ancient Tholkappium down to the latest scribbles. Those rules are not held to be obsolete, and yet all scholars from Mahamahopadyayas down to the Per Peria Thinnai Chattambiar பேர்பெரிய திண்ணைச்சட்டம்பியார் would persist in mispronouncing the alphabet. A fair pronunciation of the Tamil alphabet lingers yet with the so-called illiterate Tamils in this Presidency and the literate in the northern parts of Ceylon. The present members of the Tamil Lexicon Committee would do more active damage than the illiterates, to the most scientific phonetics of Tamil, by authoritatively recording the mispronunciations as standard in their lexicon. Their negative virtue of omitting the transliteration of the Tamil words, will be doing real good to the language. The standardising of the mispronunciation strikes at the very foundation, the philosophical basis of the language. Philosophy apart, the system of phonetics defined in the Tamil Grammars is a highly scientific one, and, if these rules are not given up, we have characters in Tamil to write any language on earth without borrowing a single letter from elsewhere. A simpler and yet perfectly scientific and all comprising system is inconceivable. The grammar of the Tamil phonetic system was dealt with in sufficient detail, demonstrating its perfection, in the Wesley College Hall on the 23rd February 1917. In the interests of our beloved language, my humble services are ever at the disposal of earnest enquirers.

In the alphabetic philosophy, the Tamil letters divide themselves into 5 classes—Panchabootha letters—viz. the three divisions of the mute consonants, வல்லினம், இடையினம், and மெல்லினம் —hard, medial and soft—the Prithvi, Appu and Theyu letters, the vowels உயிர் are the Vayu letters and the unique Tamil letter Ayda ஃ is the Akâsa letter. Just as the combination of the five elements or Panchaboothas produce the various material substances found in the universe, the correct combination of the five elements of the Tamil phonetics, Panchabootha letters, produce all composite sounds found in any language. I do not mean to convey, that the Tamil language uses all the possible composite sounds out of its alphabet. Though characters are provided in the Tamil language for all elements of articular sounds, for certain reasons which cannot be detailed now, they limited to common use, only certain composite sounds. By standardising mispronunciation, we utterly destroy the scientific utility of the system.

The Rationalistic School has, as far as this lecturer is aware, no materials whatever in this very important branch of language, apparently because the sounds are not inscribed anywhere. Fortunately the grammars define them.

The forms of letters may be considered next. For philosophical purposes, more than anything else, the forms of letters are no less important than their phonetics. For the assumed attainment of various Sidhis or acts, Mantric Chakras or amulets are used. In them, various combinations of letter forms are used, and even the cutting or such other treatment to certain parts of letters are assumed to affect adversely or beneficially the individuals with reference to whom the incantation is made. Certain Chakras or amulets have smaller letters placed at various points in and around a larger letter. All these show that in the Mantric period the alphabet had definite forms and that there were also definite conceptions and understandings as regards the forms.

The grammars, which so clearly define the pronunciation of the letters, fail to give a description of their written form in detail. The partial omission, far from implying the non-existence of writing at the time of those grammars, goes to prove the contrary. The few cursory references to forms in Tholkappium such as :—

> " ஆய்தமென்ற முப்பாற் புள்ளியு மெழுத்தோரன்ன "
> " மெய்யினியல்பு புள்ளி யொடுநிலையல் "
> " எகர ஒகரத் தியற்கையு மற்றே "
> " உட்பெறு புள்ளி யுருவா கும்மே "
> " புள்ளியில்லா வெல்லா மெய்யும் "
> " வேற்றுமை வழியபெயர்புணர் நிலையே."

place beyond doubt that writing was in vogue at the time of Tholkappium, the age of which can be proved to be not later than the 4th century B. C., distinctly prior to the time of Asoka.

In fact, the very first word of the very first Sutra or rule of Tholkappium, *viz.* "எழுத்தெனப்படுவ" means that which is written. It is most important to note that there is no term in the Tamil language based on the idea of sound to mean a letter of the alphabet. We have only பொறி and வரி as the equivalents or other names of எழுத்து in Tamil. As for the word சொல் we have no less than 31 Tamil equivalents all based upon the idea of sound *viz*.

அசைப்பு, அறை, இசை, இசைப்பு, இயம்; உரை, கரை, கிளவி, குயில், கூற்று, செப்பு, தோல், தோற்றம், நவற்சி, நொடி, பகர்ச்சி, பணி, பயில், பறை, பனுவல், பாணி, புகல், புகறல், பேச்சு, மறை, மாற்றம், மொழி, வாய்மை, விளம்பு, வினை.

If the various shades of meanings conveyed by the two words சொல் and எழுத்து are considered, no evolutionist would grumble to concede that, though the period of the language indicated by the coming into existence of the term சொல் must be chronologically far anterior to the period when the term எழுத்து came to exist in the language, the civilization of the Tamils in the எழுத்து stage must be something wonderful.

The various meanings of the word சொல் are (1) word, (2) term, (3) phrase, (4) sentence, (5) passage, (6) declaration, (7) assurance, (8) command, (9) maxim, (10) promise, (11) praise, (12) paddy, and (13) toddy.

Whereas the various meanings of the word எழுத்து are :—(1) letters of the alphabet, (2) writing, (3) a written letter, (4) an entry, (5) cyphering, (6) written accounts, (7) written engagement, (8) bond, (9) record, (10) enrolment, (11) registry, (12) delineation, (13) engraving, (14) painting, (15) literature, (16) science, (17)

Mystic or Mantric letters, (18) letters in Chakras or amulets and (19) destiny. Most of these uses are now obsolete.

It cannot possibly be gainsaid that, the age of the word எழுத்து must be far anterior to Tholkappium which uses it, and the Tamils should have been in a high state of civilization and had a written language long prior to the 4th century B.C., the lowest limit of the time of Tholkappium.

More than anything else, the philosophy of the Tamils as gleaned through Tholkappium—all literature anterior to Tholkappium having been unfortunately lost entirely—reveal a perfect scientific knowledge and renders the key of the mystic or philosophic basis of the language. The word mystic must not be misunderstood. As the *rationale* of the mystic is unravelled loop after loop and link after link, the word mystic looses its mystery and begins to signify that it only engenders more subtle laws of nature than the ordinary ones and consequently more generic in their application.

Philosophy is the Marrow of the Tamil Grammar and Language.

Even a cursory glance of that ancient grammar Tholkappium will convince that the grammatical terminology employed in it are the identical philosophical terminology necessary for dealing with the grammar of the phenomena of life. If in place of the alphabet, words, and sentences, treated in that grammar, their corresponding mystic equivalents in philosophy are substituted, the Sutras or the rules of Tholkappium expound the phenomena of life instead of the phenomena of the Tamil language. For instance:—

Vowels are called உயிர் or ஆவி meaning life or soul *i.e.* Jeevathma.

Mute consonants are called உடல் or மெய் meaning body *i.e.* Thrimalakosa or Jata

Syllabic consonants are called உயிர் மெய் meaning life or soul ensheathed in the body *i. e.* Jeevathma in Thrimalakosa.

Hard consonants are called வல்லினமெய் meaning embodiment of arrogance *i. e.* Anavamalakosa.

Medial consonants are called இடையினமெய் embodiment of illusion or duplicity *i. e.* Mâyâmalakosa.

Soft consonants are called மெல்லினமெய் meaning embodiment of temptation *i. e.* Kâmiamalakosa.

The chapter dealing with the combination of consonants is named புள்ளிமயங்கியல் or மெய்ம்மயங்கியல் meaning the illusioning of the body *i. e.* illusioning of the Thrimalakosa.

The chapter dealing with the combination of vowels is named உயிர்மயங்கியல் meaning the illusioning of souls.

The chapter dealing with the phonetics of the alphabet is named பிறப்பியல் meaning the laws of birth *i. e.* Janana.

The various treatments to which letters are subjected are described as எடுத்தல், நலிதல், படுத்தல் synonymous with Srishti, Thithi and Sankâra. The two letters வ and ய are termed "உடம்படுமெய்" meaning the body that unites soul with soul, or the form that annihilates births. The same two letters வ and ய occur in Manthras where they are termed as grace and soul letters respectively, with the aid of which the emancipation of soul or the annihilation of births is attained.

Verbs are called வினை meaning Karma. Transitive verbs are called பிறவினை *i. e.* others Karma. Intransitive verbs are called தன்வினை *i. e.* one's own Karma. Unfinished verb is called வினையெச்சம் *i. e.* unfinished Karma. Finite verbs are called முற்றுவினை or finished Karma. Symbolic verb is called குறிப்புவினை or unknown Karma. Declarative verb is called தெரிநிலைவினை or known Karma. Affirmative verb is called உடன்பாட்டுவினை or விதி வினை meaning unchangeable Karma. Verb in future tense is called எதிர்காலவினை or Akâmiakarma. Verb in present tense is called நிகழ்காலவினை or Prârathvakarma. Verb in the past tense is called இறந்தகாலவினை or Sanchithakarma. Inflection of nouns is called வேற்றுமை meaning transformation or transmigration to suit Karma.

Instead of swelling the instances of nomenclature of grammatical terms to convey philosophical sense, I may quote a few Sutras or rules of Tholkappium in which the philosophical import can be easily appreciated :—

"வேற்றுமைதாமேயேழெனமொழிப" is the first Sutra in, வேற்றுமையியல். Here is a noticeable coincidence with the Hindu philosophical principle of seven different kinds of births or transmigrations of souls, ordinarily.

"வினையெனப்படுவது வேற்றுமை கொள்ளாது நினையுங்காலைக்கால மொடுதோன்றும்" is the first Sutra in "வினையியல்" (which philosophically signifies the rules of Karma). The philosophic meaning of the Sutra is distinct. The Karma does not transform with the transmigration of souls but remains intact and lies dormant waiting for the proper time according as the Karma is Akâmiya or Prarathva or Sanchitha.

Similar idea is expressed in "வேற்றுமைவழிய பெயர் புணர்நிலையே", a Sutra in புணரியல்.

"மெய்யின் வழியதுயிர்தோன்றுநிலையே" is a Sutra in the first chapter. Its meaning is the grammatical sense in plain. The philosophical import is equally apparent. Considering the souls by themselves, there is nothing to distinguish except by their envelope, the body which asserts itself over and above the soul. Let the consonant or மெய்யெழுத்து—க் represent the body of a cuckoo and let the Vowel or soul ஊ get into that body. The resulting syllabic consonant or creature உயிர் மெய் is கூ and we see here that it is the cuckoo that coos. Let the consonant or body ம் represent the body of a cat and let the same vowel or soul ஊ get into it. The resulting syllabic consonant or creature, உயிர் மெய் is மூ and we see that though the vowel or soul உயிர் is the same in both the cases, now it is the cat that mews.

Can the principle of the body asserting itself over the enclosed soul or Jeevathma be better expressed than in this Sutra "மெய்யின்வழியதுயிர் தோன்றுநிலையே"? These are not stray instances of coincidence.

"புள்ளிமீற்று முன் னுயிர் தனித்தியலாது
மெய்யொடுஞ்சிவணு மவ்வியல் கெடுத்தே."

and,

"மெய்யுயிர் நீங்கிற்றன் னுருவாகும்"

are Sutras in the chapter புணரியல் which deals with the rules relating to the combination of soul and soul, the combination of soul and body and the combination of body and body. The philosophic import of the above two Sutras is plain. When a soul is brought in bondage with a body in any plane of existence, it is not in its nature to retain its individuality and it becomes one with the body; and when the soul departs from the body the latter reverts to its original elements.

To illustrate the coincidence of the rules relating to the letters in the grammar with the Manthric or mystic rules pertaining to the same letters in their mystic aspect, it is necessary to quote a few instances.

> " எல்லா மொழிக்கு முயிர் வருவழியே
> யுடம் படுமெய்யி னுருவு கொளல் வரையார்.'

is the Sutra or rule for the combination of two words, the end of the *standing* word—நிலைமொழி—aud the beginning of the *coming* word—வருமொழி—being உயிர் or vowels. As a rule of grammar it states that while the vowel-beginning of the *coming* word may retain its own form in the presence of the vowel-ending of the *standing* word, authorities do not restrain or impede the *coming* vowel from getting itself into the consonants ய் or வ் called உடம்படுமெய். In the philosophic sense the Sutra would mean that, while a *coming* soul or Jeevathma or Pasu in the presence of a *standing* soul or universal soul—Paramathma—or Pathi—is at liberty to retain its own form and individuality, there is no restriction or impediment for the *coming* soul—Jeevathma—to ensheath itself in one of the two special bodies ய் and வ் which are called உடம்படுமெய் or special bodies which can unite the *coming* soul or Jeevathma with the universal or *standing* soul—Paramathma or Pathi. Here the necessity arises to explain what is meant by உடம்படுமெய் in grammar as well as in mystiology, and why the two ய் and வ் alone out of the 18 consonants should be so called. The term 'உடம்படுமெய்" is popularly taken to be synonymous with "உடன்படுமெய்" and interpreted to mean the consonant which unites the vowel-ending of the *standing* word and the vowel-beginning of the *coming* word. When the mystic significance of these two important letters ய் and வ் is considered, the additional meaning of the word "உடம்படுமெய் "—உடம்பு—அடும்—மெய்—a consonant which annihilates other consonants (in grammar) or form that annihilates birth (in philo sophy) suggests itself.

The various forms of bodies or births in which the souls are entangled are treated as Thrimalakosa or embodiment of illusion and yet out of the births of Deva—godly, Nara—human, Mruga—beast, Pakshi—bird, Keeda—worm etc., the human form is considered the best and foremost preferable to even the Deva forms. For instance in Thâyumânavar's work the following stanza may be noticed.

" எண்ணரிய பிறவிதனில் மானிடப்பிறவிதா
னியாதினும் மரிதரிதுகாண்
" இப்பிறவி தப்பினா லெப்பிறவி வாய்க்குமோ
வேதுவருமோ வறிகிலேன்
" கண்ணகநிலத்து நானுள்ளபொழுதே யருட்
ககனவட்டத்தினின்று
" காலூன்றி நின்று பொழியானந்த முகிலொடு
கலந்து மதியவசமுறவே
" பண்ணுவது நன்மை................"

The reason assigned for such high reckoning of the human form is that, while the Deva or godly forms are merely intended for the enjoyment of the happiness of a fleeting nature, and the forms of beast, bird and worm are those which are defective in the possession of the sense of god or Gnâna, it is only the human form that enables one to attain the emancipation of the soul it ensheaths. The body in the physical existence, corresponds to மெய் or உடம்பு—mute consonant in the language. Quite analogous to the Narâ or human form being specially distinguished out of all Thrimalakosa the two consonants வ் and ய் are distinguished in Manthric or mystic letters as those which are essential in the incantations for obtaining the emancipation of soul—Jeevathma ய with the aid of God's Grace வ. It is important to point out here that these two letters play in Manthras a part quite analogous to that they play in the language as "உடம்படு மெய்."

The eminence of God's Grace is described in the couplet in Thiruvarutpayan "திருவருட்பயன்".

" அருளிற் பெரிய தகிலத்து வேண்டும்
" பொருளிற்றலையிலது போல்."

There is nothing more eminent than God's Grace for all souls, just as there is nothing more eminent in this world than the object one longs for.

That the mystic value of the letter ய is the soul or Jeevathma will be apparent from the couplet in the same work:—

" விரியமனமே வியவ்வை மீளவிடா சித்தம்
" பெரிய வினை தீரப் பெறும்."

which the commentator explains thus:—

"மகார நகாரமாகிய மலமும் திரோதமும் மிகவும் மிறசப்புணர்ந்து யகாரமாகிய உயிர்களைத்திரும்பவிடா ; அவ்வுயிர்கள் தம்பெரிய பிணியாகிய மலவிருள் தீருங்கால் சிகார மாகிய சிவத்தினையடையும்."

Translation:—The evil passions denoted by the letter ம, and the obscuration denoted by the letter ந, hold themselves fast to the souls denoted by ய, and prevent the latter's emancipation. Those souls, when the insuperable bondage of the three evil passions or darkness clears out, *reach* Siva denoted by the letter சி.

Pope's translation of the couplet is :—

" Ma and Na prevail over the mind, thus it returns not to him.
Whenever it obtains Ci, its deeds are cancelled."

That the mystic value of the letter வ is God's Grace, will be clear from the couplet in the same work.

" வாசியருளியதை வாழ்விக்குமற்றதுவே
" யாசியுருவமுமாமங்கு."

which the commentator explains thus : —" வகாரமாகிய அருள் சிகார மாகிய சிவத்தினைக் காட்டி, யகார மாகிய உயிரினை வீட்டின்பத்திலேயிருத்தும். அன்றியும், அவ்வருளே யந்தச் சிவத்திற்குக் குற்றந் தீர்ந்த திருமேனியாய் இருப்பது.

Translation:—The God's Grace வ will introduce the soul ய to Siva சி and lead to the enjoyment of emancipation. Further, the spotless form of Siva is the same Grace வ.

Pope's translation of the couplet is :—

" Va will in grace give Ci and bring prosperity,
To such Souls this is the spotless Form which will appear."

Thus, it will be seen, that in the mystic formula Panchakshara ஓ நமசிவய, the function of the two letters ய and வ is to bestow emancipation to eager souls—Jeevathma—in the presence of the Universal Soul or Paramathma. In the grammar of the combination of words the *standing* vowel நிலையுயிர் corresponds to the Paramathma and the *coming* vowel வருமுயிர் to the Jeevathma.

"உடம்படுமெய்" is defined by two Sutras quoted by Nachinârkiniar viz.

"உடம்படுமெய்யே யகாரவகார,
"முயிர்முதன் மொழிவரூஉங்காலையான."

Translation :—The syllabic consonants ய and வ resulting from the combination of the *coming* word which has a vowel-beginning, are called "உடம்படுமெய்."

"இறுதியுமுதலு முயிர்நிலைவரினே
யுறுமெனமொழிய வுடம்படுமெய்யே."

Translation :—If the end of the *standing* word and the beginning of the *coming* word happen to be உயிர் or vowels, the consonants called "உடம்படுமெய்" form in the combination.

The work Thiruvarutpayan திருவருட்பயன் is, no doubt, very recent. It was written after the influence of Sanskrit, well established itself in South India. The above two Sutras or rules quoted by Nachinarkiniar purporting to be from a grammatical work which was anterior to and the basis for Tholkappium, conveying the same philosophic and mystic sense with regard to the two letters ய and வ, is worthy of special note. The strangeness, is not so much in the meaning of the grammatical rule coinciding with the philosophic and mystic rules with regards to these two letters, but is in the construction of the language to uniformly obey these rules.

If the form of the letter வ is examined, the mystic importance attached to it will be apparent. Out of the monogrammic letter அ which comprises அ as the whole figure, உ as the top portion and ம as the bottom portion placed up-side down, if the head and tail of ம are severed, the remaining letter is வ (see the 5th letter அ on page 6.) Thus the letter வ in its form comprises the whole of the Linga or long stroke denoting Siva, the whole of the letter உ or Sakthi, and the mere stem or body of ம or Mala which is inseparable from the Sakthi. According to the mystic literature, the letter வ is God's Grace which liberates the soul—Jeevathma—from its three evil passions or Mala signified by ம. In the form of வ, we find the coincidence that it is the letter which is free from the main parts, the head and tail of ம, and yet it comprises the whole of the Siva and the Sakthi forms. When we identify the forms of the two letters இ and அ with the forms of the deities Dhakshinamoortha and Oorthvanatana, it will again be realised that the letter வ comprises such of the Deities' limbs that are free from Mala or impurity.

To quote another example of mystics in grammar: in the various Manthric formulæ the letters ம், ண் and ன் occur. In the transformation of letters from the letter அ, the letter ம gets one oval loop of அ, the letter ண gets 2 such loops and the letter ன gets 3. The recognised mystic value of ம when it is used as the representative of its class, is Mala or evil passion of soul in general, but in relation to ண and ன, the letter ம denotes single Mala or evil passion, as the விஞ்ஞானகலர்—Vignânakalars are subject to, ண denotes two evil passions or Malas, as பிரளயாகலர்—Pralayakalars are subject to and ன

denotes the three evil passions or Malas, as சகலர்—Sakalars are subject to. Thus in the mystic order, ம is inferior to ன and ன to ண, in their evil functions. There is further the recognised mystic principle that Mala ம vanishes on the approach of grace வ.

Now coming to the grammar of language,

"னகாரைமுன்னர் மகாரம் குறுகும்" is a Sutra in மொழிமரபு in Tholkappium, meaning that ம் becomes short **after** ன். The commentator adds,

"இனித்தன்னின முடித்தலென் பதனான் ணகாரவொற்றின்முன்னு மகாரம் குறுகுதல் கொள்க" *i.e.*, applying the same rule to allied sounds it follows that ம் shortens after ண் also.

"வகாரமிசையும் மகாரம் குறுகும்" is another Sutra in புள்ளி மயங்கியல் of Tholkappium, meaning that ம் shortens **before** வ. These two rules are combined in Pavananthi's Nannul Sutra:

"ணனமுன்னும் வஃகான் மிசையும்மக்குறுகும்."

It will thus be seen that no strain is necessary to recognise the identity between the grammatic and the mystic rules pertaining to the letters ம, ன, ண, and வ.

Perfect system in the formation of the Tamil Language.

I wish also to bring to your notice a few points illustrating the perfect system under which the Tamil language seems to have been constructed. The existence of such a system would imply, that the language was constructed by the master hand of some individual or body. This may appear to clash with the ordinary conception of the general laws of evolution of a language; but a deeper consideration will show that it need not clash, even though it is based on a perfect system which in this case happens to be a mystio-philosophic one. Treating this language as a *product*, we have only to apply the laws of evolution to the *producer*, an individual or a body that may be.

To proceed with the present theme, a few simple cases of system in the language may be quoted. The Tamil names of numerals may be compared with the names in other languages not allied to Tamil. We have the series of words ஒன்று, இரண்டு, ஒன்பது, பத்து, பதினொன்று, தொண்ணூறு, நூறு, தொள்ளாயிரம், தொள்ளாயிரத்து தொண்ணூற்றொன்பது, ஆயிரம், ஆயிரத்தொன்று, ஆயிரத்துத் தொள்ளாயிரத்துத் தொண்ணூற்றொன்பது, இரண்டாயிரம் etc. in Tamil. In English we have ஒன், டூ, த்ரீ, ஃபோர், ஃபைவ், ஃசிக்ஃச் எய்ட், ட்வெண்டி, தௌ ஃ சண்ட் ஃ etc., In Hindustani we have ஏக், தோ, தீன், சார், பாஞ்ச், சே, சாத் ஆட், நௌ, தஃச் etc. In the latter 2 languages, the names of numerals end in varying sounds, both vowel and consonant, whereas in Tamil the names systematically end in the vowel உ except when ஆயிரம் comes in when it ends in ம். We know these two letters உ and ம் are the last two of the three Pranavaic elements அ, உ and ம், which represent the Universal Soul—Pathi, the individual Soul—Pasu, and the evil passions of the Soul—Pâsa respectively.. The Universal soul—Pathi denoted by the letter அ cannot unquestionably be subjected to enumeration. Even the individual Soul—Pasu denoted by உ, which in its pure state is supposed to have no tangible form, cannot be subjected to enumeration. The abstract evil passions denoted by ம் too cannot be enumerated. When the Pasu or individual Soul உ is entangled in Pâsa there will be tangible forms which can be enumerated, that is to say, when உ gets into the Thrimalakosa or மெய்யெழுத்து—mute consonants—the உ thus entangled is countable. Does then ஒன்று mean one ௧, பத்து mean ten ௰ etc.? If this is conceded, we may look for an explanation of the ம் ending of the word ஆயிரம் in the Thirumanthiram stanzas :—

"அணுவுளவனு மவனுளணுவும்
"கணுவரநின்ற கலப்பதுணரார்
"இணையிலி யீசனவ னெங்குமாகி
"தணிவரநின்ற சராசரந்தானே."

and

"அணுவிலணுவினை யாதிப்பிரானை
"அணுவிலணுவினை யாயிரங்கூறிட்
"டணுவிலணுவை யணுகவல்லார்கட்
"கணுவிலணுவை யணுகலுமாமே."

Can then the philosophic principle adopted in the formation of the Tamil names of numerals be expressed thus?

பதிபசுபாச மெனுமுப் பொருள்களுள்
முதலதிலக்கில விடையுங் கடையும்
புணர்வுழியெண்ண லளவைக்கிணங்கலின்
எண்ணுப்பெயர்கள் எண்ணுமுகரத்தையே.

Gentlemen, you must excuse me if you think that I am taking long flights of imagination. The comprehension of the subject does require a good amount of imaginative faculty, and yet it will not be found wasted in the study of this wonderful language.

The cogent philosophic system is easily perceptible in the mute consonants. They are a speciality in this language. These sounds are irreducible to further factors. They are the very primary bodies of sounds and are 18 in number classed into three equal divisions of 6 hard, 6 soft and 6 medial letters.

These mute consonants are named உடம்பு or மெய் or உடல்,—Thrimalakosa or body, and the Tamil names of their three sub-divisions viz. வல்லினமெய், இடையினமெய் and மெல்லினமெய், are also expressive of the philosophic basis of the language. In the Panchakshara நமசிவய, there are two soft letters ந and ம, the mystic values of which are Throtha or obscuration and Mala, or evil passion respectively. Out of the three remaining letters சிவய, the last two வ and ய are distinctly medials or இடையினமெய் and these are assumed to be the letters which give emancipation. The letter சி—chi—though one of the hard consonants in the language, when used in the Manthra, it should be pronounced as a triphthong with the Ayda or Thrinethra or Siva letter ஃ as the leading letter, that is ஃ—ச்—இ makes Ci. Therefore, in the use of the Manthra, சி also becomes a medial, thus giving 3 medial 2 soft and no hard letters in the five mystic letters. In the lexicon, the proportion of Tamil words beginning with the medial, soft and hard letters is 1: 2: 8. In any Tamil work dealing with general topics, when the actual number of medial, soft and hard letters are counted, it is seen that the medials figure least and the hard letters figure most. Thus we see that what is most in the Maha Manthras is the least in use in the common language, and what is least in the said Manthras is the most in the common language. But, even in the common language, if pieces dealing with special topics are taken, we see how distinctly these three classes of consonants, medial, soft and hard or Mâya, Kâmia and Anava letters assert themselves as such and break their natural proportions. We can, with mathematical precision, measure the various degrees of Anava or arrogance expressed in pieces of work, by the various percentages of the hard letters or வல்லினமெய் found in them.

Take for instance the stanza in சடாயு உயிர் நீத்த படலம் in Kambarâmayanâ, wherein Râvana addresses Jatâyu with audacity thus :—

"சேட்டானிருதர்க் கிறை கேழ்கிளர்தன்
"வாட்டாரை நெருப்புக வாய்மடியா
"ஓட்டாயினி நீயுரை செய்குணரைக்
"காட்டாய் கடிதென்று கனன்று ரையா."

In this, the percentage of வல்லினமெய் hard consonants is 53, whereas that of both the soft and medial put together is only 47.

Where the sentiment of arrogance or Anava is of a higher pitch, for instance in the stanza in வாலிவதைப்படலம் of Kambarâmâyana wherein Sugreeva challenges Vali, the percentage of hard letters increases.

"இடித்துரப் பிவந்துபோ ரெதிர்த்தியே லடர்ப்ப னென்
"றடித்தலங்கள் கொட்டிவாய் மடித்தடுத்தலங்கு தோள்
"புடைத்து நின்றுளைத்த பூசல் புக்கதென் பயிக்கிடம்
"துடிப்பவங் குறங்கு வாலிதிண் செவித்தொளைக்கணே."

Here the percentage of the Anava consonants வல்லினம் has gone up to 64, whereas that of both the other classes of consonants put together is only 36.

In the stanza in மாயாஜனகப்படலம் of Kambarâmâyana wherein Râvana solicits Seetha to yield to his Kâma or lust, it will be noticed how the Kâmia consonants மெல்லினமெய் rise above their normal percentage and the Anava consonants or வல்லினமெய் fall.

"வஞ்சனே னெனக்கு நானே மாதரார் வடிவு கொண்ட
"நஞ்சுதோயமுதமுண்பானச்சினே நாளுந் தேய்ந்து
"நெஞ்சுநோரான தம்மை நினைப் புவிட்டாவி நீக்க
"அஞ்சினேனடிய னேனும் மடைக்கல மமுதின் வந்தீர்."

In this, the Kâmia or soft consonants bear a percentage of 47, whereas the hard or Anava bears only 36, and the medial still less, viz. 17.

I have to give you, gentlemen, at least one instance to show how,—when the sentiment expressed is holy or spiritual, when the aim is emancipation, when it is a pathetic appeal for any purpose,—the medial consonants or இடையினம் which alone own the mystic letters of emancipation, rise in percentage abnormally over the other Anava and Kâmia consonants.

"எழுவாயெவர்க்கு முதலாகி யீறேடிடையாகி
வெங்குழுளையாய்
"வழுவாதவர்க்கும் வரமீயவல்லே யவரால்
வரங்கள் பெறுவாய்
"தொழுவாயுணர்ச்சி தொடரா தன்மை யுருவாய
மறைந்தி துயரால்
"அழுவா யொருத்தனுளே போலுமாரிவ் வதிரேக
மாயை யறிவார்."

This is a stanza in நாகபாசப்படலம் of Kambarâmâyana, wherein Garuda praises Râma pathetically, when the latter was in a swoon. It is noticeable in this that the Anava or hard consonants fall down unusually to 29%, the Kâmia or soft consonants fall still low to 13% whereas the medials or இடையின மெய் rise up in a startling manner to 59%. According to

Manthric or mystic rules, the letters ய, ர and வ out of the 6 medials are those which have the efficacy of emancipation. The stanza quoted is one of the 24, which carry a legend with them, to the effect that, when these stanzas of praise were recited by the author, Kamban, over the corpse of the snake-bitten child at Chidambaram, the child revived. If we further examine the stanza to which mystic efficacy is attributed, to find the percentage of the mystic letters ய, ர, வ out of all the medials in it, we find 71% to be these letters. Again, if we strike the percentage, not on their numerical quantity but on their measure or மாத்திரை, the percentage rises to 80. It cannot be stated that Kamban intentionally swelled such stanzas with the medials or the mystic letters far above the normal percentage obtaining in the common language, though the coincidence of the high percentage of the medials and the mystic letters with the special pathos and the mystic legend of the stanza is extremely strange. Gentlemen, you are very likely to misunderstand me that I am trying to impose on you a strong conception of absolute mysticism, but I must say an emphatic on to it. I simply mean to impress that a natural law impels one to use more of the medials for expressing sentiments allied to the longing of the soul to do away with its Mala entanglement. In applying this law of pathos running with the sound of the consonants, it is necessary to discern first of all whether any one class of pathos is put on with the cloak of another. One devotee addresses his deity for *emancipation alone*, but in doing so he *asserts* that he is *entitled* to *demand* emancipation. Here, the *assertion*, *title* and *demand* immediately bring in the pathos of Anava or arrogance and the language accordingly calls into service the hard consonants வல்லெழுத்து. Another devotee personates himself as a maiden and addresses his deity as a lover. Though the avowed object is emancipation, the pathos of Kâma or lust comes in, and the language takes in more of soft consonants. Similarly various other shades of combinations of pathos occur in the use of the language without infringing the above law.

At every step we find nothing but system and order in major and minor matters alike in this language. The mute consonants க், ம், ன் etc. require a vowel beginning to pronounce them as letters, and the vowel used is invariably இ for example இக், இம், இய் etc. The Ayda letter ஃ also requires a vowel beginning to pronounce it, but in this case, instead of the vowel இ, the letter அ is used and ஃ pronounced as அஃகன்னு or அஃகேனு. This unmistakable system, which will attract any observer, is easily traceable to the mystic rules of letters. The philosophical divison of the Tamil letters are three, viz., Siva, Sakthi and Mâya or Pathi, Pâsu and Pasa letters. The Pathi or Siva letter is the Ayda or Thanynilai ஃ, the Pasu letters are the 12 vowels and the Pâsa letters are the 18 consonants. These are the primary or main divisions, but each one of them is divisible into three subsidiary parts of exactly similar classification. Thus the Pathi letter Ayda ஃ is divisible into three parts, viz., Pathi in Pathi, Pasu in Pathi and Pâsa in Pathi. In this case, the three dots of the letter signify the three sub-classes of Ayda. The top dot is the Pathi in Pathi, the right one the Pasu in Pathi, and the left one is the Pâsa in Pathi. The cogency of this division will be clear, when the form of the Ayda is eventually identified as the symbol of the Thrinethra or the three eyes of Siva, and of the three eyes, the top one is the symbol of Jothi or light, the right one is that of Surya or sun the source of energy, and the left one is that of Chandra or moon the source of Mâya or lust.

Similarly the 12 vowels, which in the main or the primary classification come under Sakthi or Pasu, are sub-divisible into three parts, Pathi in Pasu, Pasu in Pasu and Pâsa in Pasu. Out of the three letters அ, இ, உ in the sub-classification, அ is the Pathi in Pasu, உ is the Pasu in Pasu and இ the Pâsa in Pasu. On a consideration of the mystic rules, the cogency of the system of adding the vowel இ to pronounce mute consonants, and that of adding the vowel அ to pronounce the single letter Ayda ஃ will now be apparent. The mute consonants are in the main classification, Mala or Pâsa letters; and when a vowel is needed to lead them, the most suitable one is இ because it is the Mala or Pâsa vowel in the secondary classification; and so the consonants are pronounced as இக்கன்னா, இம்மன்னா, இய்யன்னா etc. For similar reasons, when a vowel is required to pronounce the primarily Pathi letter ஃ, the Mala vowel இ cannot be chosen and the principal Pathi vowel அ is used and the Ayda letter pronounced as அஃகன்னா or அஃகேனா.

Will it not be appropriate then to define these principles thus?

மும்மல வெழுத்தாம் மூவாறு மெய்யையும்
தனித்தியக்கு முயிர் இகாரமென்க
தனிநிலை தானே யியங்காதமரிற்
தனித்தியக்கு முயிர் அகாரமென்க.

From this we can proceed to discern the system or order underlying some of the more specific and internal structure of the language. We have in Tamil three letters அ, இ, and உ called சுட்டு or demonstratives, corresponding to the English expressions *that*, *this*, and *something between that and this* to express the last of which there is no single word in English. The vowel sound அ in the word *that* corresponding to the Tamil demonstrative அ, and the vowel sound இ in the word *this* corresponding to the Tamil demonstrative இ are noteworthy. The three demonstrative letters are unique in Tamil. They happen to be the very three Pathi, Pasu and Pâsa letters in the sub-classification of the main Pasu letters or vowels. Out of these three, the vowel இ is the one which actuates the pronunciation of all the 18 mute consonants or Mala letters. The Mala letters are represented by ம் in the Pranava ஓ. If we substitute ம் in place of இ in the three demonstratives, we get the complete set of the Pranavaic elements அ, உ, and ம் denoting respectively the same Pathi, Pasu and Pâsa as before. The meaning of these three demonstratives is in keeping with the philosophical conception of the three objects viz. Pathi, Pasu and Pâsa mystically denoted by these letters. Pathi or Lord or Universal Soul is that which is as distant to conception as it is to come in communion with and the letter அ which in mystiology denotes Pathi, in the language as a demonstrative points to that which is far off. Pâsa or Thrimalakosa or body is that which is at hand, and which can be easily but falsely realised as self and which can be pointed out as *this*; and the letter இ which in mystiology denotes Pâsa or Thrimalakosa or body in the language as a demonstrative means that which is at hand. Pasu or Jeevathma or individual soul is that, the existence of which can be easily perceived by any one unlike the Universal Soul, and yet cannot be easily realised or pointed out as tangibly as the existence of the body or Pâsa, and is therefore one which in the normal conception is neither so far as the Universal Soul nor so near as the Thrimalakosa or body and the letter உ which in mystiology denotes Pàsa or individual soul, in the language as a demonstrative means the thing which is between *that* and *this* or which is neither far nor near. It should not be thought that I am mystifying the Tamil demonstratives, அ, இ, and உ. On the contrary my endeavour is to de-mystify, that is to deduce the *rationale* of the mysticism already enshrouding these demonstratives. The Sutra in Tholkappium as regards these is:

"அ, இ, உ, அம்மூன்றுஞ்சுட்டு"

which Ilampooranar interprets thus: "குற்றெழுத்தென்னப் பட்டவம்மூன்றுஞ் சுட்டென்னுங் குறிய வென்றவாறு."

Nachinarkiniyar interprets in the same way and adds a note thus "இதுவும் ஆட்சியும் காரணமும் நோக்கியதோர் குறி, சுட்டி யறியப்படும் பொருளையுணர்த்தலின்."

Translation:—This (the name சுட்டு) is also a *mark* குறி distinguishing the domination and reason, because (சுட்டு) signifies the objects which are worthy of being known.

I have quoted both Ilampooranar and Nachinarkiniyar and added a translation of the latter's note to show that the conception of both these commentators, as regards the name of the demonstrative letters சுட்டு, was plunged in mysticism. The mysticism and importance attaching to the word சுட்டு are not confined to its usage in Grammar. "பிறரால் பெருஞ்சுட்டு வேண்டுவோர்" in ordinary language means, one who wishes to be praised by others, and so சுட்டு in this phrase means praise; again, சுட்டுப்பொருள் in the ordinary language means "the image of a deity formed in the mind at pleasure, the god appearing in that form, as a guru, either mentally or occularly, according to the proficiency of the worshipper." சுட்டு வைக்க means "to form an image of the deity in the mind, as the object of worship, the external senses being all restrained and the attention fixed on that only."

The following amplified Sutra will clearly bring out the mystio-philosophical significance of the demonstratives so far explained:—

சுட்டத் தகுபொருள் மூலமுப்பொருளை
அவையுட் பதிதான் அகாரமாகும்
உகாரம் பசுவாம் மகாரமெய்ப் பாசமாம்
மகார மெய்யை யியக்கும் இகரத்துடன்
அ, இ, உ அம்மூன்றுஞ் சுட்டே.

To quote one more instance: it is not impossible to pronounce a word which has a mute consonant as its first letter in any language, and in fact other languages abound in such words, expressing elevated as well as depraved ideas. For instance, the following words may be compared:— Bliss, blemish; Christ, crime; Druid, drunkard; Friar, fret etc. in English and Sri, Srartha; Krupa, Kroora; Prarthana,

Prayaschitha ; Brahma, Brashta ; etc. in Sanskrit. Were the Tamils physically incapable of pronouncing any word with a mute consonant as the first letter? What other rational cause compelled them to frame a rigid rule to the effect "உயிர் மெய்யல்லன மொழிமுதலாகா"? The rigidity of the rule does not stop with their own words. When they borrow from another language a word which begins with a mute consonant, before it is admitted into the fold of their words, the foreigner is subjected to a sort of Prayaschitham (purification) and a vowel is grafted as part and parcel of the head of the foreign word, for example:—Krupa or க்ருப (Sanskrit) and Kirupa or கிருப (Tamil) ; Mruga or ம்ருக (Sans) and Miruga or மிருக (Tamil) and so on. We know in the phenomena of life alone that a dead body cannot lead an organised congregation. The Tamil grammarian named his mute consonants as dead bodies—உடல்—and the vowels as life or soul—உயிர்—in the language. Unless it was his specific intention to apply the laws of life to the language, it is hard to account for such a ruling as "உயிர் மெய்யல்லன மொழிமுதலாகா," meaning *viz.* no body devoid of life can lead an organised congregation.

It will not be out of place here to mention, that the principal Tamil grammars include as an important and indispensable chapter பொருளிலக்கணம் or the grammar of *objects* and *objectives* which gives quite a unique feature to the Tamil grammars. The great importance attached by the ancient Tamils to such inclusion of *objects* and *objectives* in the grammar of their language, cannot but indicate that they were striving to identify the laws of general existence with the laws of grammar of the language. Irayanâr Agapporul—இறையனார் அகப்பொருள்—is a work recognised on all hands to be an ancient one, and belonging to the Sangam period of Tamil. The legendary author of the work is Siva, the God himself. The circumstances piously attributed to its composition will bear quotation from its commentator, Nakkirar, a leading Sangam poet.

"அரசனும் புடைபடக் கவன்று, 'என்னை? எழுத்தும் சொல்லும் யாப்பும் ஆராய்வது பொருளதிகாரத்தின் பொருட்டன்றே! பொருளதிகாரம் பெறேமேயெனின் இவைபெற்றும் பெற்றிலேம்' எனச் சொல்லா நிற்ப, மதுரை ஆலவாயின் அழநிறக்கடவுள் சிந்திப்பான். 'என்ன பாவம்! அரசற்குக் கவற்சி பெரிதாயிற்று. அதுதானும் ஞானத்திடைய தாகலான் யாம் அதனைத் தீர்க்கற்பாலம்' என்று இவ்வறுபது சூத்திரத்தையும்செய்து, மூன்று செப்பிதழகத் தெழுதிப் பீடத்தின் கீழிட்டான்."

Translation:—The king deeply regretted and exclaimed 'are not the studies of the chapter on the letters, words and prosody in grammar merely subservient to the study of the chapter on the *objects* and *objectives*; and if we have not got this latter chapter, the possession of the other chapters is not worth anything. The bright complexioned God of Alavâi (Madura) duly considered and pitied for the king's sorrow, and felt that as the sorrow was due to a craving for divine intelligence He is bound to remedy it. Thereupon He (the God) composed these sixty Sutras, wrote them on three copper plates and deposited them under the seat."

Nakkirar's commentary seems to have interpolations of a later date, and yet there is no reason to suppose that the above legend is such an interpolation. If this legend does not serve

1 Median Sectional view of the brain

2. Horizontal Section of brain

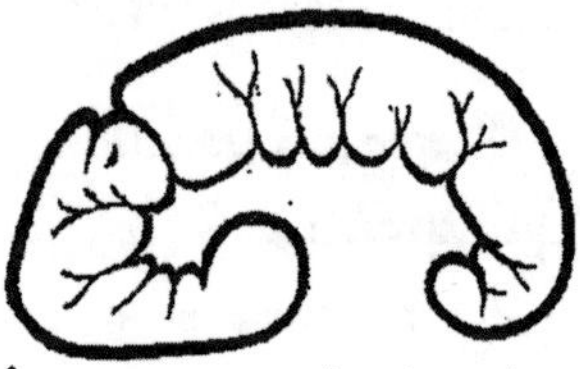

3. Half Section of spinal cord

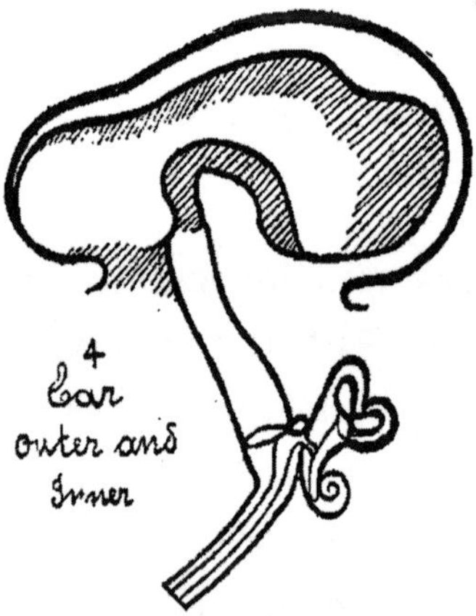

4 Ear outer and Inner

6 General view of Liver Stomach and Intestines

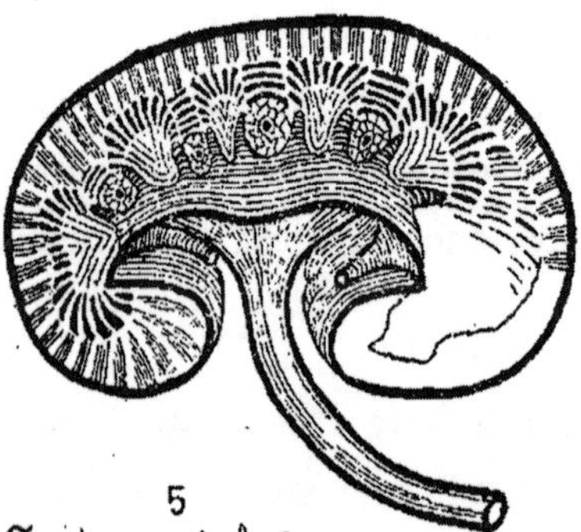

5 Section of kidney

any useful purpose to the historian, does it not add one more solid piece of evidence to prove that the ancient Tamils, unlike others, rightly or wrongly, treated the phenomena of language to be categorically analogous to the phenomena of general existence in the universe?

The coincidence of natural forms with the epigraphist's constant and the mystic's sheet-anchor ஓ.

I have till now, dealt with two distinct varieties of coincidences viz., that of the transformation of letters and that of the structure of the language, with the Hindu mystic-philosophy. The letters, the language, the mystics and the philosophy are all considered as the products of man, *i.e.*, as artificial. I now proceed to demonstrate some equally strange coincidences of those products of man with the products of nature or God, if you choose to call so, or in other words the coincidences of that, epigraphist's constant and the mystic's sheet anchor ஓ, with the natural forms. Let us commence with the human physiology our nearest concern. If we observe with a critical eye, a certain unmistakable uniformity and rhythm in the forms of organs can be easily perceived. Page 48 shows diagrammatically the pictures of some of the most important human organs. The pictures are adopted from the recognised anatomical charts. Fig. 1 is the median sectional view of the brain. If the outline of this is traced clock-wise, commencing from the frontal brain—the *cerebrum*, thence passing round the small brain—the *cerebellum*, thence to the *medulla oblangata* and thereon along the spinal cord, the form of a beautiful ஓ is obtained. Even the inner details of the section exhibit the main outline of ஓ in various phases. Figure 2 is an horizontal section of the brain. This too presents, in outline as well as in details, the main parts of ஓ. Figure. 3 is the half section of the spinal cord which too has a remarkable coincidence with the main features of ஓ.

Figure 4 shows the external and the internal human ear. If the outline is traced clock-wise, commencing from the lobe of the external ear, thence along the edge, next through the channel tothe inner ear, thence to the labyrinth and back and on along the *eustachian* tube, another beautiful picture of ஓ is obtained.

Figure 5 is the longitudinal section of a human kidney. The coincidence of its outline with the form of ஓ is apparent. Various other human organs, each of which performs a definite unit function, such as the spleen, the lungs, the pancreas, sweat glands etc., exhibit similar delineation in their general form. Figure 6 shows in a group the liver, the stomach and the intestines —the trinity of digestion—each one of them intended to do a definite function. The general semblance of the liver to ஓ, and of the stomach to ஓ placed upside down, is noticeable. The most remarkable concidence is in the disposition of the intestines. This long and flexible organ measuring over 30 feet and comprising the small and the large intestines, is fixed to the back wall of the body on a particular plan, though one would think that it can be heaped up in any manner within the walls of the abdomen. The small intestines are coiled up and placed in a central position analogous to that of the spiral-beginning of the letter ஓ. The ascending colon, the transverse colon, the descending colon, the inflexion and the rectum complete the form of ஓ.

The evolutionists have established beyond dispute the general agreement existing between the human and other animal organs. They have further established, that the agreement is stronger and stronger as the animal in its physiology approaches nearer and nearer the human species. Therefore, it only remains for me to point out that the basic form of the organs of all the animals including man seems to be ஓ, the semblance becoming more and more perfect as the animal approaches the human species.

The coincidence does not end here. If the development of the human embryo is traced from the time of its inception to that of its parturition, as diagrammatically illustrated on page 53, the gradual development and the ultimate perfection of the form of ஓ cannot fail to attract the attention of anybody. Figures 1 to 6 are adopted from Parker. The semblance of ஓ becomes more and more striking as the embryo developes. The head of the embryo occupies the place of the spiral right loop of ஓ, the lower half of the body that of the left loop, and the umbilical cord with the placenta that of the stem and the slanting stroke of ஓ. In *Figure* 1, the umbilical vesicle occupies almost the whole space. In Figures 2, 3 and 4, the umbilical vesicle gradually diminishes; in Figure 5 the cord is distinct and only the trace of the vesicle is left; and in the fully developed child Figure 6 the cord and the placenta only remain.

Though the child straightens up after birth, if it lives to old age, the disposition to revert to the original ஓ shape sets in strongly; at first, the person simply droops, but ultimately he developes the perfect humpbacked ஓ form as illustrated in Figure 7.

Even in embryology, the evolutionists have placed beyond doubt that the embryonic form of all creatures is alike in the earlier stages. I have therefore only to say that this stereotyped form, so much depended upon by the evolutionists to establish their theory, very remarkably coincides with our wonderful ஓ.

On page 56 the various stages of the development of fœtal membranes of a bird are diagrammatically shown. In Fig. 1, the umbilical duct is not distinctly developed and hence the semblance of the form is only partial ஓ. In Figs. 2 and 3 the development of the umbilical duct is more perfect and the resemblance of the forms to ஓ is also more perfect.

A series of 8 embryos *viz.* that of fish, salamander, tortoise, chick, hog, calf, rabbit and man in three comparable stages of development are shown in pages 54 and 55. In the third or the lowest series in the picture, the identity of the animals offer no difficulty whatever. In the first and the second series, identification by mere appearance is impracticable. In the first series the agreement of the forms of the various animals is remarkably perfect. Their coincidence with the form of ஓ is equally perfect. The umbilical vesicles and the placenta are not shown in these diagrams and hence their ஓ form is short of the stem and the slanting stroke.

Another interesting coincidence in these embryos is the number of folds in their neck with the number of letters in the

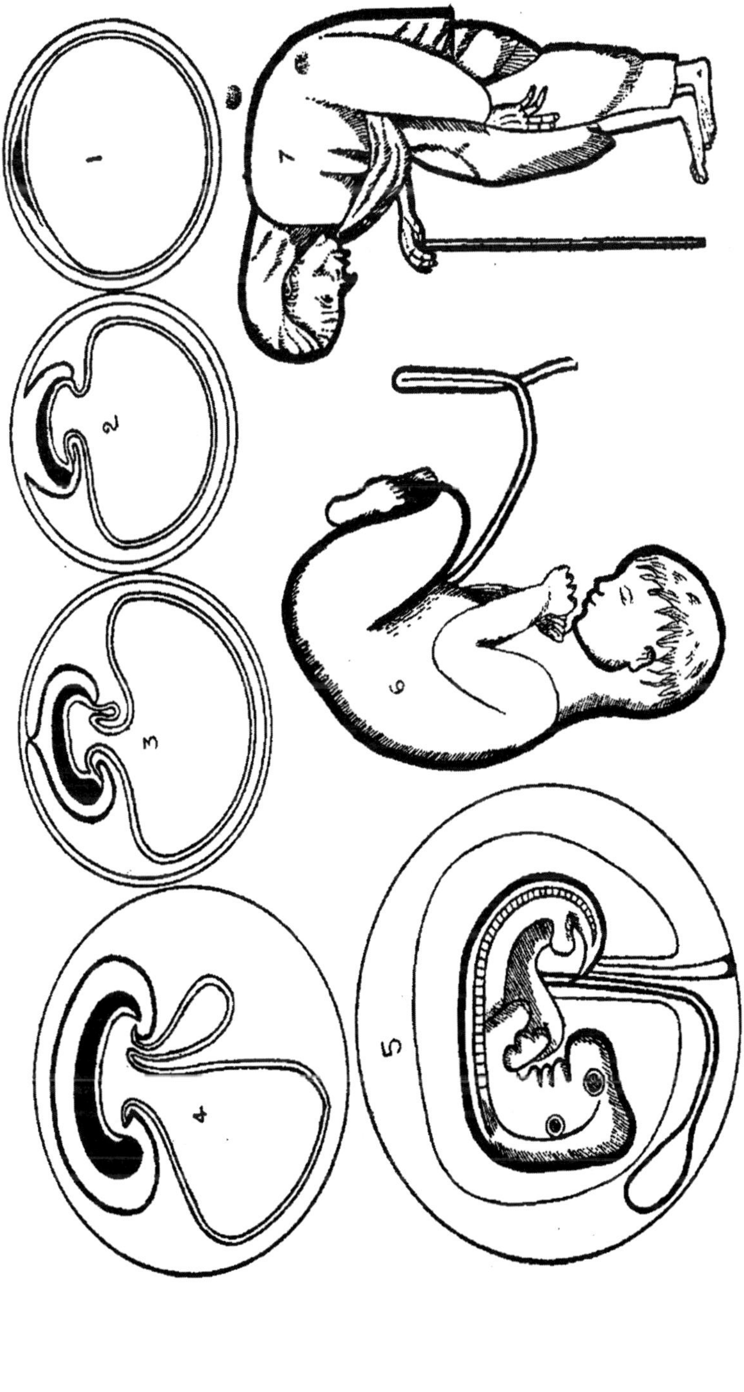
1
2
3
4
5
6
7

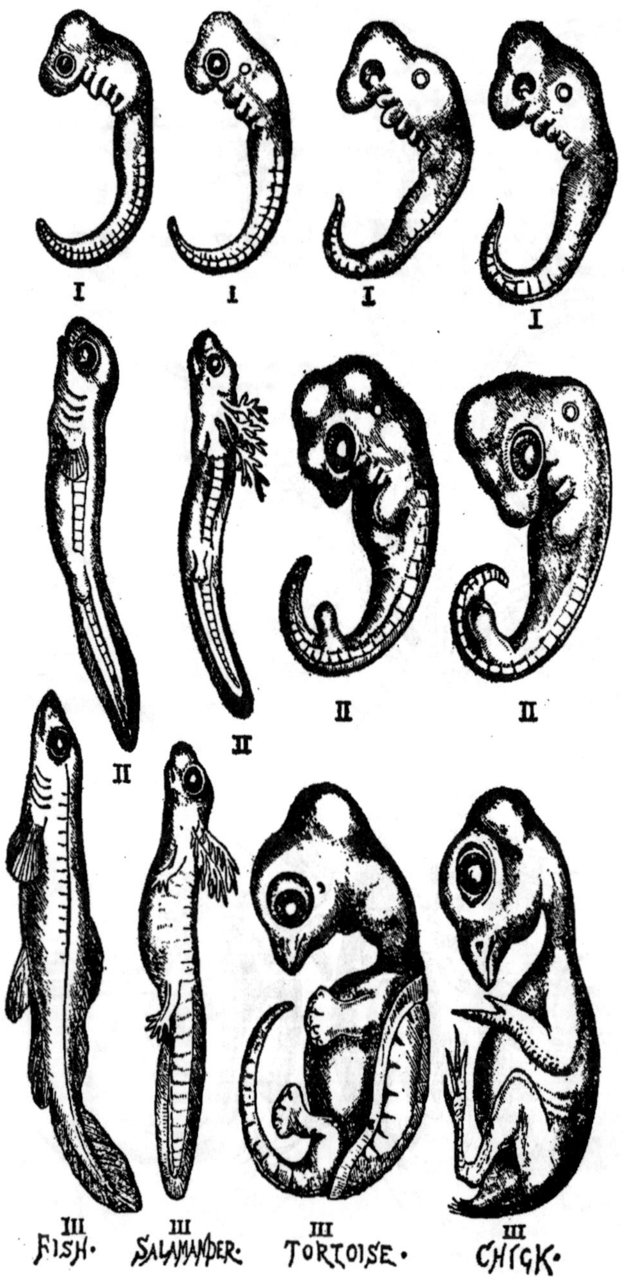
I
I
I
I
II
II
II
II
III
III
III
III
FISH.
SALAMANDER.
TORTOISE.
CHICK.

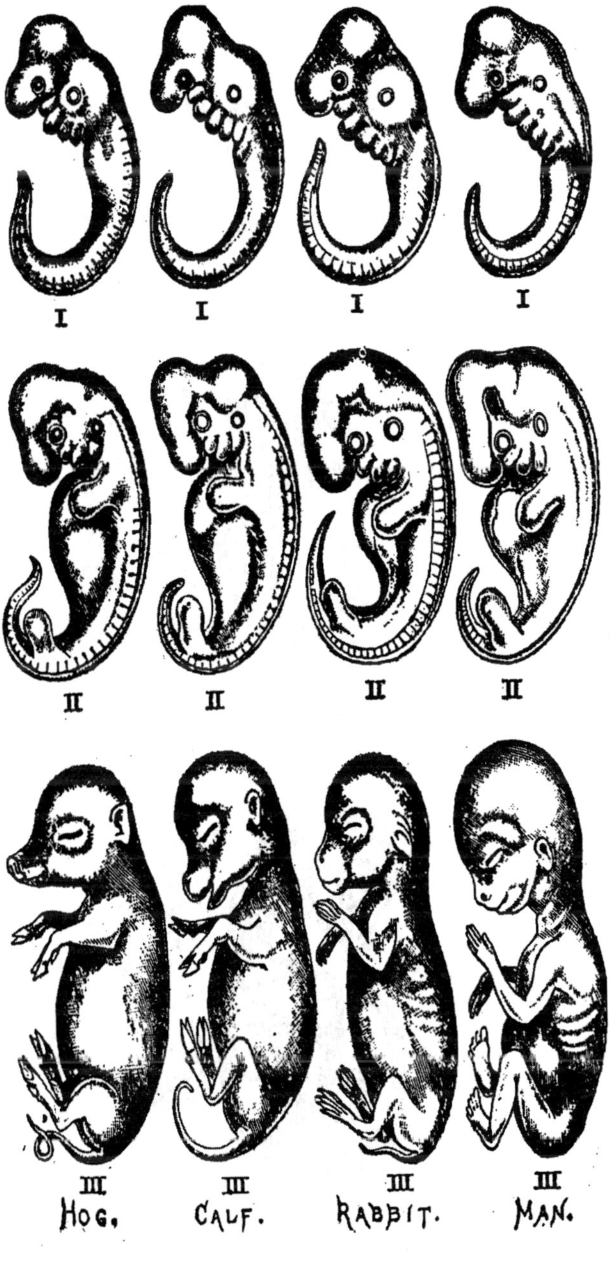
I
I
I
I
II
II
II
II
III
HOG.
III
CALF.
III
RABBIT.
III
MAN.

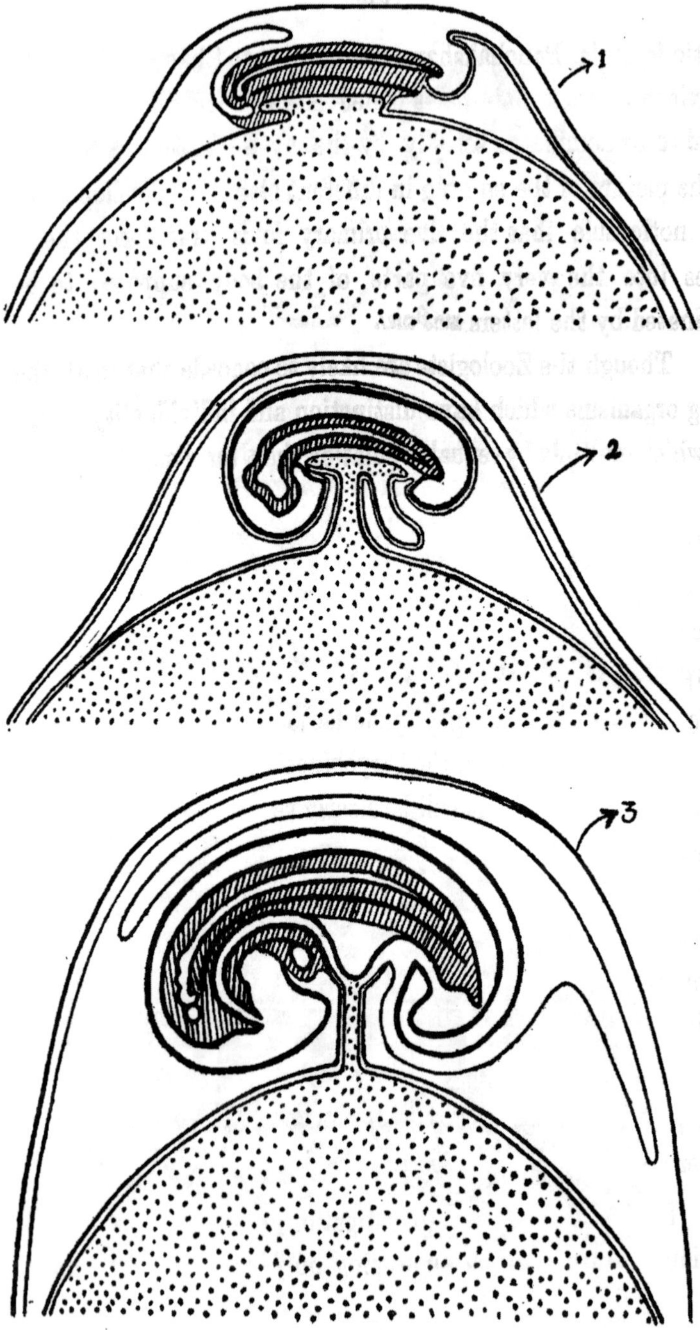
1
2
3

mystic formula, Panchâkshara. According to Shâstras, the body is divided into six main parts called Āthārās and these are supposed to be dominated serially by the mystic letters ஓ நமசிவய. In the picture of the embryo in different stages of development, it is noticeable that the five primary folds transform themselves into the very five parts of the body supposed to be dominated by the letters நமசிவய.

Though the Zoologists are likely to concede that in all the living organisms which have distinction and individuality of sex and which multiply by sexual copulation the ஓ form may be treated as the basic one, they may question how that form can apply to the unicellular organisms which multiply by mere division. Other than the amœba, the animal cells, the congregation of which produces the higher organisms, come under the class of unicellular organisms which multiply by division. Therefore, this class of life is far from being a negligible factor in existence.

If a careful study of the karyokinesis in the process of their multiplication is made, it will be clearly seen that the successive phases, in the formation and arrangement of the chromatin loops and of the nuclear spindle till the division of each cell into two takes place, present forms in the disposition of the chromatin fibres approaching ஓ more and more as the time for the division of the cell also approaches.

Even in the impregnation of the ovum, a similar process takes place, but these are too technical to deal with in any greater detail here.

It is found in the investigation, that in all cases of individual organic forms expressing only one sex, the simple form of ஓ is identifiable; whereas in the organic forms like the amœba and flora which possess the potentiality of both the sexes in one body, the superposed form of two letters ஓ, so that the two spiral loops of the two letters oppose each other, is identifiable. There are many interesting details in the application of the ஓ form to the vegetable kingdom, which, to save time, I reserve for another occasion.

In any case the inorganic world cannot be left totally unnoticed with reference to the ஓ forms. There are a number of theories about the origin of planets. Whatever may be the points of difference in them, in the two points *viz.*, that the sun and the planets formed part of one mass (nebulae) and the planets condensed and solidified themselves into their present shape and conditions in course of time, they agree. Taking the points of agreement as basis, it can be mathematically shown that the primary course of every particle in a planet was a spiral, with the sun as the starting point.

As for the ultimate individual particles of matter, the latest researches of scientists indicate that energy units of two opposite signs whirl one round the other in a manner similar to the planetary motion.

Therefore, a presumption that in the inorganic world one couple of two units describes the primary part of ஓ will not be far-fetched.

To summarise: the complete ஓ form is found as basis in the organic world whenever the sex is separately expressed in one individual: the superposed form of two letters ஓ is found in the organic world when the potentiality of the two sexes are involved in one and the same individual; and lastly the incomplete form of இ is found in the inorganic world in general.

Were the Tamils cognizant of the mystic-philosophic basis of their language?

I have quoted coincidence after coincidence which I hope will at least puzzle the most pessimistic of the evolutionists and oblige him to partially heed the remonstrance and to put cross queries. My ambition is nothing more, and if I had excited inquiry in the field of my research I have had the fullest reward and satisfaction for my labours.

I have given numerous details of the mystic-philosophic basis of the language, which, while agreeing with the recorded principles in our literature find no direct or open mention in any of them. Therefore, I may reasonably anticipate the pertinent question, 'were the Tamils ever cognizant of the mystic-philosophic principles now pointed out to be the probable basis of the language', and if the answer is in the affirmative, 'why did not they expound the same in detail?'

There are indelible evidences to prove their cognizance. The great sacredness usually attached to the mystics seems to have compelled our sages to reserve this knowledge for communication by word of mouth—Upadesa to select disciples. It is a well-known fact that such reservation still exists amongst the Indians. It is also an equally known fact that much of the valuable lore of the Indians has suffered degeneration and extinction thereby. An accidental demise of one Guru before he could communicate to his disciple, causes an eternal gap in the line of communication by word of mouth. However, it is a matter for rejoicing that the language contains indestructible land marks of this mystio-philosophy, so that we are in a position to recover the valuable lore to a great extent.

As regards the letter அ:—Thâyumânavar writes in his பொருள் வணக்கம் thus:—

" அகரவுயி ரெழுத்தனைத்து மாகிவேறு
யமர்ந்ததென வகிலாண்டமனைத்துமாகிப்
பகர்வன வெல்லாமாகி யல்லவாகிப்
பரமாகிச் சொல்லரிய பான்மையாகித்
துகளரு சங்கற்ப·விகற்பங்களெல்லாம்
தோயாத வறிவாகிச் சுத்தமாகி
நிகரில் பசுபதியான பொருளை நாடி
நெட்டுயிர்த்துப் போன்பால் நினைதல் செய்வாம்".

In this he compares the supreme *objective*, in all its attributes, to the vowel அ which he describes as the one which forms all the other letters and yet stands different from them.

Again in his எந்நாட்கண்ணி he writes thus:—

" அவ்வுயிர்போ லெவ்வுயிருமான பிரான்றன்னடிமை
எவ்வுயிரு மென்றுபணியாம் செய்வ தெந்நாளோ!!!"

meaning:—Is there a day when I may realise, that like the vowel அ, the Supreme Lord is the Master of all Souls, and serve Him?

In the well-known work சிவஞானசித்தியார் the letter அ is compared to Siva thus:—

"அக்கரங்கடோறுஞ் சென்றிடு மகரம்போல நின்றனன் சிவனுஞ் சேர்ந்தே."

meaning that the Siva's relationship with all Souls is similar to that of the letter அ which goes into every other letter.

In Thiruvarutpayan, the Lord is compared to the vowel அ thus:—

"அகரவுயிர் போலறிவாகி யெங்கும்
நிகரிலிறை நிற்கு நிறைந்து"

meaning that the Lord, who has no equal, stands paramount and all-pervading similar to the vowel அ.

Thiruvalluvar in his famous work Thirukkural, writes the first couplet for the work under the chapter கடவுள் வாழ்த்து—The praise of God:—

"அகரமுதல வெழுத்தெல்லா மாதி
பகவன் முதற்றேயுலகு."

which Pope translates thus:—

"A as its first of letters every speech maintains;
The 'Primal Deity' is First through all the world's domains."

From these quotations it will be clear that the best of our sages from the ancient Thiruvalluvar down to the recent Thayumanavar gave unreservedly to the letter அ, all the attributes they would give to the supreme god of their conception.

It is usual to contend that, in all these, that for the pronunciation of anything the opening of the mouth is essential and that opening virtually produces the அ sound, is the only point of comparison. If a proper study of the phonetics is made, it will be seen that the mute consonants which number three-fifths of the Tamil alphabet cannot use up for their pronunciation the whole of the letter அ at all. This disagreement will nullify the comparison altogether, unless the sound of அ is divided into its 3 component parts due to the three necessary modulations called எடுத்தல், நலிதல், and படுத்தல்—Srishti, Thithi, and Sankāra—starting, running and stopping of the pronunciation of the letter அ which are represented by the three Pranavic elements அ, உ and ம் and the last of them viz. ம் is applied to the pronunciation of the mute consonants. As this threefold division is indispensable to justify the comparison of the letter அ with the Supreme God and as this same threefold division leads to numerous deductions I have drawn in my investigation, it will not be inappropriate to credit the authors I have just now quoted with the conception of the general sway of the letter அ in the language.

Thirumoolar, who seems to come more under the class, Sidhars than under Sidhantis, would say that ஓ is நமசிவய, ஓ is all other letters and in brief ஓ is everything in the universe. For instance see the following:—

"ஓமெனு மோங்காரத்துள்ளே யொருமொழி
ஓமெனு மோங்காரத்துள்ளே யுருவரு
ஓமெனு மோங்காரத்துள்ளே பலபேதம்
ஓமெனு மோங்காரமொண் முத்திசித்தியே.

ஓங்காரத்துள்ளே யுதித்தவைம் பூதங்கள்
ஓங்காரத்துள்ளே யுதித்த சராசரம்
ஓங்காராதீத் துயிர் மூன்று முற்றன
ஓங்காரம் சிவபர சிவரூபமே.
பழுத்தன வைந்தும் பழமறையுள்ளே
விழித்தங் குறங்கும் வினையறிவாரில்லை
எழுத்தறிவோ மென்றுரைப்பர்களேதர்
எழுத்தை யழுத்த மெழுத்தறியாரே.
அங்கமுமாகம வேதம தோதினும்
எங்கள்பிரா னெழுத்தொன் றிலிருப்பது
சங்கை கெட்டவ் வெழுத் தொன்றையுஞ் சாதித்தால்
அங்கரைசேர் ந்தவருங்கலமாமே ".

The Sidhanti's 14 Shastras would also say in the same manner that ஓ is everything. For instance :—

" இறைசத்தி பாசமெழின் மாயையாவி
யுறநிற்கு மோங்கா ரத்துள்."

(Thiruvarutpayan)

Thâyumânavar the latest would also say so. For instance:—

" நீங்கர் துயிருக்குயிராகி நின்ற நினையறிந்தே
தூங்காமற்றூங்கினல்லாதே யெனக்குச் சுகமுமுண்டோ
வோங்காரமா மைந்தெழுத்தாற் புவனத்தை யுண்டுபண்ணிப்
பாங்கா நடத்தும் பொருளே யகண்ட பரசிவமே."

But these are reckoned to be recent works when compared with those of the Sangam and the pre-Sangam days. Unfortunately we have no works of those days now extant which deal with religion, and consequently we have only to seek side-lights thrown by the extant works.

We have, however, one work Thirumurugatrupadai of Nakkeerar, which is devoted to the praise of God Muruga and the antiquity of which is not disputed. In this, naturally one cannot expect to find an exposition of அ and உ. But in one of the stanzas subjoined to this work and attributed to Nakkeerar, he seems clearly to identify the Siva's five faces with the Muruga's six.

"அஞ்சுமுகந் தோன்றில் ஆறுமுகம் தோன்றும்
வெஞ்சமரந் தோன்றில் வேல்தோன்றும்—நெஞ்சி
லொருகானினைக்கி லிருகாலும் தோன்றும்
முருகா வென்றோதுவார்முன்."

The meaning of this may be controversial but in the body of the work, the following two lines occur and reveal indisputably the state of religion of South India in Sangam times.

"மந்திரவிதியின் மரபுழிவழா
அந்தணர் வேள்வி யோர்க்கும்மே யொருமுகம்."

meaning :—One face (ஓர் முகம்) would deeply consider (ஓர்க்கும்மே) the sacerdotal oblations (வேள்வி) of the Anthanars or god's devotees (அந்தணன் means god*) who never deviate (வழா) from the Manthric rules (மந்திரவிதி) as obtained by tradition or ancient usage (மரபு).

---

* See Thiruvalluvars'-Kural.
"அறவாழி யந்தணன்றாழ் சேர்ந்தார்க்கல்லால்
பிறவாழி நீந்தலரிது" wherein அந்தணன் means god

I have already quoted from Thiruvalluvar on page 18

"நிறைமொழி மாந்தர் பெருமை நிலத்து
மறை மொழி காட்டிவிடும்."

in which மறைமொழி or the Secret Word is referred to.

In the above we have enough evidence to know that in Sangam times (close to the time of Christ) that Manthras (மறை மொழி, மந்திரம்) and sacerdotal oblations (வேள்வி) existed and that they were most piously safeguarded from exposure to the common populace. Numerous instances of a similar nature can be quoted from Sangam works. Epigrâphical records also confirm the same. For instance பல்சாலை முதுகுடுமிப்பெரு வழுதி, a Pandyan King who ruled probably in the 1st century before Christ, owes his name to the numerous Vedic sacrifices performed by him.

Tholkappium itself, which is recognised to be anterior to the third or last Sangam period, records this sort of mysticism and thus betray that the mystics were dominant in those as much as in later times. In மரபியல் we find the Sutra:

"நிலந்தீ நீர்வளி விசும் பொடைந்துங்
சலந்த மயக்க முலக மாதலின்
இருதிணையைம்பா லியனெறிவழா அமைத்
திரிவில் சொல்லொடு தழாஅல்வேண்டும்."

In this the combination of the five elements—Panchaboothas is plainly referred to as Maya, fully in keeping with the mystio-philosophic import demonstrated in this paper.

Tholkappiar winds up பிறப்பியல், which deals with the origin of the alphabetic sounds, in his Sutra:

'எல்லா வெழுத்தும் வெளிப்படக்கிளந்து
சொல்லிய பள்ளி யெழுதரு வளியிற்
பிறப்பொடு விடுவழி யுறழ்ச்சிவாரத்
தகத்தெழு வளியிசை யரிறப நாடி
யளபிற் கோடலந்தணர் மறைத்தே
யஃதிவ ணுவலா தெழுந்து புறத்திசைக்கும்
மெய்தெரி வளியிசை யளவு நுவன்றிசினே.

Here the author Tholkappiar distinctly avows that what he writes about the origin of the letter sounds, is that which is outwardly or materially realisable by the ordinary people, that it is usual in the Secret Science of God (அந்தணர் மறைத்தே) to discern the internal or mystic origin of letter sounds from the navel region of the body, and that he does not deal with this latter in Tholkappiam.

As already noticed, he names the first sub-chapter which deals only with the number, names, forms, and classification of letters as "நூல் மரபு." This very significant nomenclature is commented upon by all commentators from Ilampooranar and Nachinarkinar down to Arasan Shanmuganar. It will become too tedious if they are quoted here. It is enough to mention here that they widely differ about its significance.

The word நூல் means (1) thread, (2) carpenter's line, (3) a Brahmin badge, (4) a wedding badge, (5) deliberation, (6) literature, (7) science, (8) Sacred learning, and (9) Vedas.

Compare.

"அருணூலுமாரணமுமல்லாது மைந்தின்
பொருணூல் தெரியப்புகும்."

where அருணால் means Veda. The word மரபு means (1) antiquity (2) nature, and (3) established usage.

There is no doubt the chapter deals with 'the established usage' மரபு of something denoted by the word நால். The combination of the first 6 meanings of the word நால் with 'the established usage' மரபு will give *prima facie* absurd results. A combination of 'the established usage' with the 6th and the 7th meanings, namely, *literature* and *science*, may appear to give some sense, but when we consider that the other chapters which deal with words etc. will also be entitled to such appellation, we are driven to the necessity to enquire what particular distinction the subject of this chapter has to warrant the appellation. The only two other meanings of the word நால் being 'Sacred learning' and 'Vedas' we have to seek explanation in these two only.

I have endeavoured to identify ஓ in the natural forms; I have shown the transformation of ஓ into அ and அ into ஓ and I have also shown the transformation of அ producing the various Moola Manthras. I have further deduced from the forms of letters the mystic-philosophic principles which are usually recognised by Indians. If it is further possible to identify the form of the Pranavaic letters அ and ஓ in the form of the deities worshipped by the South Indians, the interpretation of the word நூல் மரபு as the established usage of Sacred learning or Vedas will not be objectionable. Further, by applying the process of transformation of letters it is found as already demonstrated, that the word நூல்மரபு is produced by the re-arrangement of the parts of 4 letters அ *i.e.*, ஓ, the very four letters which are supposed to have produced the Vedas.

The Tamil alphabet book called அரிசுவடி is also one which deals with the number, names, forms and classification of letters just as நூல்மரபு. I have also demonstrated that the word அரிசுவடி also emanates by the transformation of 4 letters அ *i.e.*, ௐ. In view also of the fact that any and every word in Tamil is not transformable to use up all the parts of an integral number of letters அ, we have to consider these titles with great concern. It is only when these two words retain their form of natural combination (இயல்புப் புணர்ச்சி) as அரி சுவடி and நூல் மரபு they are deducible from four letters அ; but if they undergo change of letters (விகாரப் புணர்ச்சி) in the combination as அரிச் சுவடி, and நூன் மரபு they are not so deducible.

The well known legend relating to the imprisonment of Brahma by Muruga who gave four knocks on Brahma's four heads which boasted to have produced the four Vedas from four Pranavas, seems to have an apparent bearing on the Arichuvadi and Nulmarapu, because the Vedic and Scientific principles are deducible from the forms and other features of the letters dealt with under those two titles. The title அரிசுவடி is a combination of the two words அரி and சுவடி. This title is wrongly derived by some from the first word in "அரி ஓம், நன்றாக, குருவாழ்க, குருவே துணை," found in the first page of the alphabet book similar to the derivation of the title "ஆத்திச்சூடி." The word அரி is the one which has the largest number of meanings in the Tamil lexicon. In its various meanings it includes the principal Gods, Siva, Vishnu etc., and all the principal elements and actions in nature a knowledge of which is worth acquiring. Therefore, the title அரிசுவடி seems to be a very comprehensive one. It seems to announce that the contents of the book viz. the Tamil alphabet, signify in their form and principle universal knowledge. The invocation to Vinâyaga in the same book *viz.* " அரி வரி யிரகசியம் அறிந்து கூறவே, கரிமுகனிருபதம் கருத்துளிருத் துவாம்.". avows plainly that there are secrets (இரகசியம்) in the forms (வரி) of the letters. Therefore the attempt to deduce the secret significance of these letters is neither a far-fetched nor an unwarranted one. I have made elaborate study of the mystio-philosophic significance of the letters treated in Arichuvadi and Nulmarapu but, I have to reserve their exposition to another occasion.

Now I shall close this part of the lecture by inviting your attention to the picture on page 70. I am sure you will at once say it is a huge letter ஓ. If the faint lines in the picture are deciphered, the Dhakshanâmoortha form of Siva will appear. Of course, the picture was specially prepared so that the outline of ஓ may arrest the eye of the onlooker, and yet no deviation has been made from the orthodox delineation of the God's figure. If the present day artist looks at the picture, he would at once condemn it as inartistic, as the various limbs are placed in impossible positions and if one attempts to sit in that pose he will at once have an attack of cramp. I don't mean to say, gentlemen, that, because the impious man tries to imitate God's posture, he is punished by the Divine will. I mean only that it is physically impossible to sit in that posture. Probably, it may be possible if one rehearses constantly like the circus players. I have already shown see pages 2 and 3, that by turning the stem and the slanting stroke of ஓ 180 degrees, the letter அ forms. The stem and the slanting stroke of ஓ correspond to

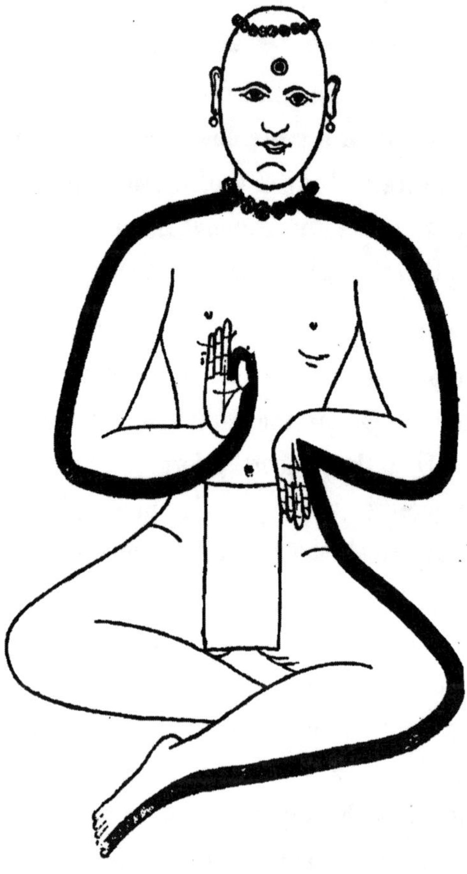

the left leg of God Siva. The turning of the left leg of Siva vertically upwards is in what is called the Oorthvanatana form

The Oorthvanatana form is another still more impossible posture. These two unnatural postures delineating the *resting* and the *acting* or the potential and the kinetic forms of nature corresponding to the letters ஓ and அ respectively seem to have been permanently impressed on the God's figure for reference and veneration. It is worthy of note here that the child in the womb retains the ஓ form or Dhakshinâmoortha form, whereas after delivery and while lying on its back it folds up its leg as in the Oorthvanatana or அ form and sucks the great toe.

In the Dhakshinamoortha or ஓ form, Siva is supposed to be at *rest*. Correspondingly in Manthras, the Pranava ஓ is used for attaining emancipation and *rest*.

In the Oorthvanatana or அ form he is supposed to perform the five functions viz. Srishti, Thithi, Sankâra, Throbava and Anugraha or creation, protection, destruction, obscuration, and emancipation.

Here I wish to bring to your special notice that the outline of the letter ஓ in the Dakshanamoortha leaves out the most principal part of God's form, the head. If you recollect now that according to the Tamil grammars the letter ஒ (short O) should have a dot over it, you will at once realise that the dot is to represent the head of the god and see the *rationale* of the author or authors of Tamil having allowed a dot over a vowel. Further, the shape of the dot also gets determined by the picture of god. It must be a long one, broad at top and narrow at bottom. Ethnologists may question me whether Siva was dolichochephalous. I wish to meet in detail the numerous questions similar to these that will be excited in the Rationalistic School separately.

The right hand of the God's figure is called the Abayâstha. It can be shown that in the secondary division of the alphabet the letter அ, the first of the vowels, occupies the Abayâstha and the last letter ஔ, ends in the right shoulder. Next comes the Ayda letter, the Thrinethra or the three eyes of God ஃ, in its corresponding position in the alphabet book, *viz.*, after the vowels and before the consonants. The consonants start with க் on the left shoulder and ends with வ் in the left hand—Varadhâstha.

The remaining consonants *viz.* ழ், ள், ற், ன், occupy the left leg of God. On the left thigh and embraced by the left hand of God sits Parvathi coloured dark and all the Maya letters or consonants are on this side.

With this data it is possible to discern the various potentialities signified by the various parts of the ௐ form which seems to be generic in the universe. I have applied this criterion to discern the functions of the various organs in the animal physiology and found that the results tally startlingly well with the results already obtained by materialistic research in the west. It is even possible to peep at the secrets of such organs the functions of which are yet to be ascertained by material research. I shall close this for the present with a short address to those concerned with the various branches of study I had to touch in dealing with my subject viz., the Tamil alphabet and its mystic aspect.'

Address to those Concerned.

Having set forth the leading points of my research, it is now incumbent on me to address a few words in the way of exhortation to those concerned. To the Mystics I have to say that my exposition has no pretention to any Divine message, and that it is not meant to advocate any particular school of philosophy such as Vedhanta, Sidhanta, Visitathuvidha or Agnosticism. We have enough data to premise that there is an indelible substratum of some definite system of philosophy in the structure and the grammar of the Tamil language. A critical study of our ancient grammar, the Tholkappium, will enable us to discover that philosophy. I do not claim any credit for the suggestion. Even the Sanskritists have held a similar reverential view in regard to their grammars. To quote one instance:—In Chandogya Upanishad, Nârada says to Sanathkumâra thus :—" I know the Rig Veda, sir, the Yajur Veda, the Sâma Veda, as the fourth the Atharvana, as the fifth the Ithihasa Purana, the Veda of the Vedas (grammar); the Pitrya; the Rasi etc."

As far as my investigation goes, the philosophy underlying or incorporated in the Tamil language, embraces in full the main principles of all the six schools of Hindu philosophy including Kapila's Sankya philosophy and Pathanjali's Yoga philosophy and establishes their relative position and unity. My conclusion may be wrong but that does not lessen the interest in the subject. Let the philosophy of the Tamil language be allied to Islamism or Zoroastrianism of Christianity or anything else, and yet it is a matter of great interest to discover what it is. Such a discovery will be a valuable asset even to the historians and archæologists, as that will add a new link to their chain. Wherever I have quoted from any particular source for illustrating coincidences between the details of the philosophy of the Tamil language and those of an existing school of philosophy, it should not be presumed that I mean to guarantee similar coincidence with all the other details of the same school. The particular instance quoted only shows that that particular point is common. It is the interest of the advocates of particular schools of philosophy to investigate, in view to find whether the Tamil philosophy is their own or not.

For the real lovers of the Tamil language and people, the investigation should be of paramount interest. That able North-Indian scholar Dutt speaks of a small band of Aryan settlers in the Indus valley some 3,000 years ago, of their manly habits of living without caste barriers as they exist to-day, of their next expansion into the Gangetic valley and the aryanisation of the aboriginal inhabitants there, of the aryanisation of the Maharattas next, and of the aryanisation of the South-Indians last. According to Dutt, the aryanisation of the last mentioned took place at a period when the steel walls separating the various castes did not exist, when the intrinsic value of each individual practically determined his caste and when the Dravidas had a civilisation of their own. Even should Dutt's description of the aryanisation be true, the real Aryan *corpus* in South-India must now be next to nothing. *A cranial study* of the various classes of the South-Indians will also confirm the same. The lecturer, being a non-Brahmin, wishes to leave nothing to be misunderstood.

His best and tried friends are mostly Brahmins and he is a sincere admirer of them. There is no denying the fact that the ancestors of the present Brahmins were the most cultured among the South-Indians at the time the said aryanisation took place and hence got crystalised into a class revered by the people. As the cultured sons of the common mother Tamil, is it not their legitimate duty to own their kinsmen and to co-operate and uplift the less lucky brethern, if they have real patriotism for the welfare of our country? On the contrary, the general disposition of many a Brahmin is to disown his kinship with the rest of his Tamil brethern, to disown his very mother Tamil and to construct an imaginary untainted Aryan pedigree as if the Aryan alone is heaven-born. Dutt himself complains of what he calls patriotism of even the western scholars who have a bias to trace the original home of the Aryans to Babylon or near the Baltic Sea. The few historians, archæologists, and epigraphists we have in South-India are all Brahmins, and we must be proud of their erudite discourses. However, their general trend is to assume that they are themselves Aryans and not Tamils and to take as an axiom that Tamil and Tamils owe everything to Sanskrit. At least one of them is explicit in his endeavour o establish page after page and chapter after chapter, untainted Aryan pedigree for the Brahmins and Brahmins alone among the South-Indians. As such, he has naturally no scruples to say that the Tamils have nothing excellent or high which can be claimed as their own. Whatever is bad in them is their heritage and whatever is good they owe to Sanskrit. In answer to Dr. Caldwell's observation that in one department at least, that of ethical apothegms, it is generally maintained that Sanskrit has been outdone by Tamil' the author above referred to is " inclined to think that the existence of so many works on the ethics of daily life is an indication of the low state of morality among the early Tamils. Because it was the Dravidian whose teeth were blunted by the eating of flesh.

> கொல்லையுழு கொழு வேய்ப்பப்பல்லே
> யெல்லையுமிரவு மூன்றின்று மழுங்கி
>
> *Pat II*—117.

that required the advice,

> அருளல்லதி யாதெனிற் கொல்லாமை கோறல்
> பொருளல்லதவ்வூன்றினல்.——*Kur.*"

In his zeal, he has however forgotten that after all he has not decried the greatness of Thiruvalluvar's work, but has run amok amidst the Tamils generalising on the description of a no-class Tamilian of that age. It would have been fair if he had quoted side by side the couplet from the same *Kural.*

> " அவிசொரிந்தாயிரம் வேட்டலி னொன்றன்
> உயிர் செகுத்துண்ணாமை நன்று"

and demonstrated equally graphically the fact that the Brahmins, the topmost class who ate the flesh of all animals in thousands under the guise of Vedic sacrifices required this advice from a Valluva Pariah, a no-class Tamilian. If he had avowed that he is a Tamil of Tamils, if he had owned his unlucky mother Tamil and yet made these observations, there will then be at the best the credit of confession, which too is due to a wrong conception.

Is not the rationalists' motto that the past should be judged with the aid of the present, and the unknown should be judged ith the aid of the known? If so, we have before us the present anding instance of aryanisation by infusion of blood. It is only the Pariahs, the lowest, who submit themselves to be elevated in that manner and they produce the present Aryo-Tamilian or the Eurasian race of South-India. Even as a matter of sentiment which will not be found opposed to history, we will do well to consider aryanisation by culture and not by blood, and try to retain the integrity of the Brahmin and the Non-brahmin. The influx of the Aryan band from Central Asia into the Indus valley and their further migrations are not questioned. Were they aboriginal to Central Asia? Geologists tell us, that so late as the end of the Tertiary epoch, the whole expanse from the Chinese shore to the North Sea including the present Central Asia was one ocean and that the Central Asian tableland and the Himalayas were elevated long ages after the archaic beds of the South-Indian Peninsula came into existence. That the habitable condition of South-India dates back several geological ages beyond that of Central Asia and North-India can be verified even by a layman easily by comparing the elevations of the deltas of the Cauvery, the Krishna, the Godavery and the Ganges above the sea level. Though the Cauvery is a small river, the head of its delta is over 250 feet above the sea, whereas those of the other three larger rivers range between 36 and 60 feet, showing thereby the hoary antiquity of the South-Indian peninsula. Zoologists and Palaeontologists tell us that, in the development of species, South-India ranks clearly the first. They tell us further that the most probable home of the *homo* or generic man in the world was the submerged Tamilagam or Límuria. If terrestrial life started so early as the Archæan era in South-India under the most congenial climatic conditions for development of species, and went on developing without interruption by any serious geological commotion down to this date, and if such life started so late as the early Quarternary era in Central Asia under climatic conditions not so congenial to a rapid development of species it is hard to conceive how the Aryans sprang up there in Central Asia indigenously. Long after the great geological commotion at the end of the Tertiary era by which Central Asia was elevated the Quarternary man should have migrated gradually from South-India towards Central Asia. There was a minor commotion of the earth within historical times causing the further loss of the Southern peninsula into the sea and the elevation of the Central Indian plateau.

This last commotion should have broken the continuity of the Indian race for a very long time, during which the northern section developed independently their Aryan culture and the southerns their Tamilian culture, till the northern section moved both towards south and west. Therefore, and on other linguistic grounds which I wish to deal with in detail as a separate subject, it is very likely that there was first an efflux of the South-Indians to Central Asia before the unquestionable influx of that section back to the south. If this efflux be accepted, the numerous differences between the various migration theories can be easily reconciled.

The historical fact that anterior to Sankarâchâria, Ramânuja, Meykandadêva and others, that is anterior to the 9th century A.D., no Tamil work on philosophy proper is forthcoming, cannot be denied; but if the philosophy underlying the structure of the language itself as revealed by Tholkappium, a work anterior to Kapila's Sankya philosophy and to Pathanjali's Yoga philosophy, is appreciated, one could easily see that what we now have as the Tamil literature is only that which belongs 'to the Dark age of Tamil', whereas the real Augustan age of Tamil should have been anterior to Tholkappium.

The rationalists cannot but admit that the first grammar of any language must be chronologically posterior to its literature. The grammar and literature then continue to act and react continuously on each other, till a stable equilibrium of the language is reached and the language itself is systematised and made strictly subject to its grammar. Such a fixity of conditions we find in the Tholkappium. The most remarkable part of it is that philosophy and natural sciences are symbolised in the very alphabet and the structure of the language. Did Sanskrit itself attain such fixity at the time of Tholkappium? I hope the rationalists will not object to admit that Tholkappium is anterior to Pânineeyam. How much of Tamil literature of all kinds including philosophic and scientific works should have existed and how many stages of grammars should have existed before Tholkappium to justify the existence of this perfect grammar? Can any one say with any shadow of reason that the Sanskritist brought his culture, made the Tamil grammar out of it, and foisted it on the already existing Tamil language. Tholkappiar was a Tamil Anthanan no doubt, but even granting he was an Aryan Brahmin, all his Sanskrit culture could have helped him only to analyse intelligently the Tamil language as it existed. Its condition as it existed and as recorded in Tholkappium shows that it was in a wonderfully perfect state. Therefore, instead of bemoaning deeply for the irretrievable loss of our most valuable treasures anterior to Tholkappium in the merciless Indian Ocean, is it proper for a Tamil Anthanar to make, incomplete statements such as:—" it is extremely doubtful whether Tamil literature would be as extensive as its Sanskrit compeer":—and " original works in Tamil are not very many and they can be counted on one's finger's ends," and thus give a wrong hue to the status of the language?

We are proud to see that Dutt, who is impartial, recorded boldly in his monumental work, " the ancient civilization of India," that Panini's Sanskrit grammar is the best in the world. In what ecstacy would he have been if he had only known Tholkappium and the Tamil language?

I have to point out here that, to appreciate the real merit of Tholkappium and Kural, or to draw any historical inferences from them, one should read the texts without the commentaries. All the commentators, belonged to an epoch at least 1200 to 1500 years after the authors of the works themselves lived, and were fully imbued with the latest Sanskritist influence and had no acumen for historical research. They let in a flood of matter extraneous to the texts, which can only give us an insight into the history of the times in which the commentators lived.

It is often contended that Sanskrit, as an inflectional language, is superior to Tamil, an agglutinative one. This comparison of two dissimilar things is fallacious. If these two languages should be compared, some common points must be chosen for comparison. At least in one point *viz.*, stability, this language cannot be excelled by the other. While this can claim at least contemporaniety with Sanskrit in their youth, it can claim to its credit stability and everlasting life. If its agglutinative structure gave it its strength and unchanging youth, let us be content with it. As regards its agglutinative character, I have to add as the result of my researches that it is not only agglutinative in the formation of its words but is so to its very core. My demonstration of the transformation of the letter அ to produce the other letters of the alphabet would have convinced you also, at the same time, that the letter forms themselves are agglutinative. My demonstration of the philosophy of the letters and the language recognising the triple elements and their combination in various proportions as the phenomena of the visible or the materially realisable universe, would also have shown that the underlying philosophy of the language too is agglutinative. The philosophy of the language, as I have said before, embraces the main principles of all the six schools of Hindu philosophy. It only recognises Vedantism as the ultimate condition, just beyond the pale of the material universe.

It is necessary to touch, though briefly, the social institution of the Tamils as revealed by our grammar. Dutt has to deduce a series of inferences from the Vedic and other Sanskrit literature as regards the state of society at the various epochs in

Northern-India, whereas we have in Tholkappium the bulk of the text describing directly the state of society and castes in Southern-India so that we have no need to stand on mere inferences. It gives five territorial divisions such as குறிஞ்சி —hilly, மருதம்—plain, முல்லை between the first two நெய்தல் —sea shore பாலை—water less waste and four professional castes such as அந்தணர்—the pious, அரசர்—the rulers, வணிகர் —the traders, and வேளாளர்—the agriculturists. Scholars summarily dispose of the four fold professional classification of the South-Indians by saying that it is an adoption from the Aryans and that only the five-fold territorial classification is indigenous to the South-Indians. Whether the ancient South-Indians adopted it from the Aryans or that the Aryans or Northern-Indians adopted the same from the South-Indians, developed it in a fanatical manner like the Moplahs and their Islamism and re-imposed the same on the South-Indians later on, is not a matter past controversy at all. Let that stand apart, but it is essential here to mention that Tholkappium does not at all deal with the four-fold professional classification as categorically different from and unconnected with the five-fold territorial distinction. The four-fold professional classification is used invariably by Tholkappiar in conjunction with the five-fold territorial division foı standardising the numerous துறைகள் or themes in his பொருளதிகாரம் or the grammar of *objects* and *objectives* which forms in fact the bulk of Tholkappium. If the four-fold classification were to be expunged from Tholkappium as exotic, the whole of பொருளதிகாரம் must vanish. He further places the four-fold professional classification under மரபு or established usage. Therefore, if this was adopted from the North-Indians at all, it should have been long prior to Tholkappium. An enquiry into the probable date of adoption will lead to interesting anomalies for the historians to solve. If we read the text omitting Nachinarkiniar and other commentators for reasons already stated, we see that a transmutable, plastic and barrier-less professional distinction is all that is in Tholkappium. The Tholkappiar's fourth class, Vellalah, the noble heritage of a nation in the words of Thiruvalluvar, can never at all be identified with the degraded North-Indian fourth class Sudra of any age. The cultured or the competent section of the Vellalahs can even enter into vocations allotted to the upper three classes. A caste system nearest to this can only be found in Dutt's Rig-Vedic castes. Manu's compound castes cannot be gleaned the least in Tholkappium. Did then the adoption of the four-fold classification take place in the Vedic epoch itself? Rig Veda knows very little beyond the Indus valley. If the adoption took place in the Vedic age, did the Tamils possess perfect literature, grammar, philosophy together with the art of writing in the Vedic age, when the North-Indians owned nothing of that sort? To avoid dilation, I would answer this question by simply exhorting the historians, and archaeologists to study the text of Tholkappium divesting it of the commentaries and divesting themselves of prejudices, and I assure them that they will never have to regret the labour.

Whatever may be said about the inferences drawn by the Epigraphists from the valuable heaps of materials they have collected from stone inscriptions and copper plates, the materials themselves cannot be passed over without any attempt to reconcile them with the principles inculcated in this paper. This part of the subject cannot be summarily disposed of and it needs another lengthy discourse, but at least to announce my cognizance of this 'Ass's bridge' over which alone my subject must pass, I wish to mention a few important points pertaining to epigraphy here.

Other than Asoka's Pali edicts of the 3rd century B.C., we have got a good number of what are called Vatteluthu records on stone and plates. As far as I am aware, they all date after the Pallava occupation of Thondai-mandalam. They cover a period of about 3 centuries from the 8th to the 11th centuries A.D. The latest of them agree more with the present form of the Tamil alphabet and the earliest differ most. These lead to a natural and simple inference that the present form evolved out of the Vatteluthu, and this is the view held by most of the epigraphists. The epigraphists are, however, a little bothered by the existence of Tholkappium, which clearly signifies that there was writing before it was composed in or before the 4th century B. C. The early European scholars who investigated the subject with the meagre materials they then had, believed that there was no Tamil literature before the 8th century A. D. With the present materials, they cannot fix a date later than the 1st century A. D. to Thiruvalluvar's *Kural*, and they must recognise that Tholkappium was anterior to *Kural*. Thus they are driven to the indispensable necessity to bridge the tremendous gap of over 1000 years between Tholkappium and the earliest known Vatteluthu. One erudite scholar has attempted to identify the Vetteluthu as the script of the Tholkappium period, depending mostly on Nachinarkiniyar's commentary. As already noticed more than once, this latter lived after the use of the Vatteluthu was given up practically, and so he was under a worse category than we now are in, as he had no acumen for historical research at all. Another learned scholar has endeavoured to trace the evolution of the Tamil alphabet from the Asoka's Pali script itself to Vatteluthu and thence to the present form of the alphabet. The European scholars will have no scruples whatever to give up their Phoenician and Chaldean theories when the religio-philosophic import of the forms and the language is made known to them, as they are all agreed to concede indigenous origin to anything which has a religious import attached to it. Therefore, the local Vatteluthu theories alone have to be met. If the text of Tholkappium is read without the commentary, there is absolutely nothing to connect the Vatteluthu with it. Between Tholkappium and this date, we have a chasm of at least 25 centuries to bridge across to get at the வரிவடிவு or the written form of the alphabet. The Vatteluthu is a foreign made bridge of a very short span of about three centuries. Any endeavour to cross this wide chasm with the aid of the Vatteluthu bridge, which can barely cover less than an eighth of the expanse, will be a feat more remarkable than the legendary Hanuman's leap across the sea. Still the existence of Vatteluthu must be explained.

The art of inscription on stone and plates seem, to be entirely exotic to South-India. It was introduced by the Pallavas who were Sanskritists and who were ignorant of the Tamil language. The inscriptions examined by me show two distinct features. One set of them can be discerned to be inscriptions to dictation made by Pallava workmen who knew more of Pali than Tamil. Another set is discernible to be inscriptions made by Pallava workmen who knew no Tamil whatever, but only copied from palm leaf scripts. It is not at all true to say that the present form of the Tamil alphabet did not exist in the earlier inscriptions. The present form of almost all the vowels and consonants with only the reasonable modulations due to handwriting are found from the earliest to the latest of the inscriptions mixed up with pure and modified Pali characters with the only difference that the mumber of letters which agree with the present forms and which are found in the earliest inscriptions is very small, and that the number increases in the later inscriptions. Thus the question reduces itself to one of tracing out not the evolution of the form of letters, but of tracing the evolution of the percentage ranging from nil to cent. per cent. of letters of the present form in the inscriptions. Or, in other words, the problem is one of the evolution of the foreigner's writing of the already fixed forms of the Tamil alphabet.

Letters such as ஓ for which Pali had no forms, and letters like உ for which Pali had almost similar forms, did not suffer misproduction by the foreigner very much, but the other Tamil letters for which Pali had definite but different forms had a miserable fate. In the earlier inscriptions, these letters were represented mostly by the Pali forms and scarcely by the correct Tamil forms. Later on the Pali characters themselves degenerated by their association with the more extensive Tamil, and eventually the Tamil characters prevailed ousting the Pali altogether, quite similar to the absorption of the conquerors, Normans by the more numerous Anglo-Saxons in England. In fact, the conquerors, Pallavas themselves, were similarly absorbed so that they went out of existence here. The foreigner who is obliged to handle the local language, learns earlier to speak than to read and write that language, and his natural tendency is to transliterate the local language in his own characters. My suggestion may appear to be strange, simply because it is put forth for the first time. I myself caught the first idea from a humorous incident in our feeding choultry, where the persons fed had to write down remarks as to the treatment they received from the staff and to the quality of food they were served with. One Telugu man who knew more Telugu than Tamil left an amusing Tamil record in the choultry book the transliteration of which in English is, 'Paruppu chôru bhâga irundudu. Pâyasam môrkolambukoodâ nasâ irundudu. Chaththarathu ayyiru romba nallavuru'. This was written in Telugu characters intermixed with Tamil. Even these Tamil characters at first sight appeared in style to be Telugu, but on scrutiny were found to be Tamil. I felt that we were rewarded for the charities straight off by giving us the clue for solving the Vatteluthu puzzle. If this solution is correct, it will be more appropriate to call it Tamil Ketteluthu— தமிழ் கெட்டெழுத்து instead of Tamil Vatteluthu. I experimented thereon on this basis, in view to reproduce the Vatteluthu-evolution of about 3 centuries in a miniature of 3 weeks, by obtaining day by day the writing of a few persons, who knew no

Tamil to start with and who were coached up with Tamil writing day by day during the experiment. The result of the experiment is very interesting. I have a lot of other data too obtained in the course of my investigation all of which I would like to include in a separate paper.

The linking of the Dakshanâmoortha and the Oorthvanatana forms of Siva with the mystic-philosophy of the antic Tamil may appear to be an anachronism to the historian. If these are historically later forms, is it not reasonable to deduce that these personifications were evolved out of the abstract mystic-philosophy of the letters and the language? In fact, the innumerable forms of ceremonials and rituals, social customs and manners, the designs of dwelling houses, schools, choultries, temples etc., the location of various deities in temples, the various Pradakshanas and Appradakshanas prescribed in worship, the disposition of various dishes on a leaf for eating, the mode of sitting and eating, the various forms of Nàmaskâras of males and females, the observations of widowhood, the forms of reception in feasts and funerals, the forms of Deepârâthanâs, the use of various colours for various ceremonials, the Rechaka, Pooraka, and Kumbaka respiratory exercises in Yogic practice, the use of ayda ஃ, Vowel உயிர் and consonant மெய் letters and the use of அ, உ and ம் for the yogic practice, the forms of Yogic postures called Āchaṇâs, the adjustment of the limbs of corpses before *rigour mortis* sets in in a particular form and planting Linga stones over the buried corpses, and every other minute detail in the daily life of Southern-India for which strict rules are prescribed, are not emperic and irrational as they were believed to be

One and all of them are uniformly, cogently and most rationally based on the Tamil forms and their philosophy, with an intelligence that surpasses human conception. To describe them in detail and to explain their scientific truths will cover many treatises. It is my desire and anxiety to render my jottings in a readable form when circumstances permit. If the historian thinks that the above forms and rules are later developments, it is still better proof of the existence of the mystio-philosophy in the letters and the language which alone and nothing else can cogently, uniformly and rationally account for the evolution of these forms and rules of South-Indian life. Nachinarkiniar, who belonged to the 11th or the 12th century A. D. believed in the mystio-philosophy of the Tamil letters. In his commentary of the 1st Sutra of Tholkappium, he writes "இவற்றுட் தன்மையும் வடிவும் நமக்கு உணர்த்தலாகாமையின் ஆசிரியர் ஈண்டு உரைத்திலர்" meaning that because the form and the nature of letters should not be revealed to us the author has not dealt with them here.

Again under the Sutra "மெய்யினியக்க மகரமொடுசிவணும்" Nachinârkiniar writes "அகரமுதல" என்னுங்குறளான் அகரமாகிய முதலையுடைய எழுத்துக்களெல்லாம் அதுபோல இறைவனாகிய முதலையுடைத்து உலகமென வள்ளுவனார் உவமை கூறிய வாற்றானுங், கண்ணன் எழுத்துக்களில் அகரமாகின்றேன் யானே யெனக் கூறிய வாற்றானும் பிறநூல்களானும் உணர்க. இதனான் உண்மைத் தன்மையுஞ் சிறிது கூறினாராயிற்று."

The religio-philosophic nature so clearly attributed here by Nachinârkiniar to the letters is worthy of note.

The last and yet not the least exhortation is to all learned scholars, who value knowledge, to favour me with their criticism and suggestions on the subject. It is by wide criticism that any research can be perfected. Criticism may be in good spirit or otherwise and yet it will invariably benefit the research, while one in good spirit will elevate the critic as well. For instance, one of the Madura Sangappulavars—our pillars of the Tamil language—who happened to be a Tamil Anthanar, confronted me seriously with the question: "How could Tamil boast of all this philosophy which evolves out of the Pranava while the Pranava itself is not its own, because, according to the Tamil grammars அகர உகரம் ஔகார மாகும் or அ+உ will make ஔ and so (probably algebraically) அ+உ+ம் will make ஔம் and not ஓம்."

I may suggest one more Sutra which is similarly opposed to my mystics:—அகர உகரம் எண்பத்திரண்டே, அகர வகரம் எட்டேகாலே. and another algebraical equation of letters *viz.* அ+உ= ஔ=அவ். Therefore உ=வ்.

The emanation of such a criticism from an avowed pillar of Tamil, appears incongruous; but it is an unquestionably intelligent and learned one and is most useful for my research. I do not propose to answer it here and prolong further. Individual human knowledge can never be perfect and so irrespective of all care and industry I have bestowed, errors in details are likely to have crept in, particularly because this paper was got ready at a very short notice, though the foundation of the subject is a very strong one. This paper will suggest numerous questions and most of these will be the very questions that occurred to me in my researches, for, the process of research itself is raising questions and finding solutions. As this paper is too brief for the vastness of the subject, numerous points had to be left without mention. The interwoven nature of the subject militates against piecemeal treatment of individual questions. I have, therefore, to earnestly solicit my learned readers to kindly communicate to me the various queries and suggestions that occur to them which I shall acknowledge individually and embody *en masse* in another paper. I close this discourse wishing prosperity for the Tamil language, the Tamil people and the Tamil land with which, I hope, all my hearers and readers will heartily join, and reminding you of the Universal Letter.

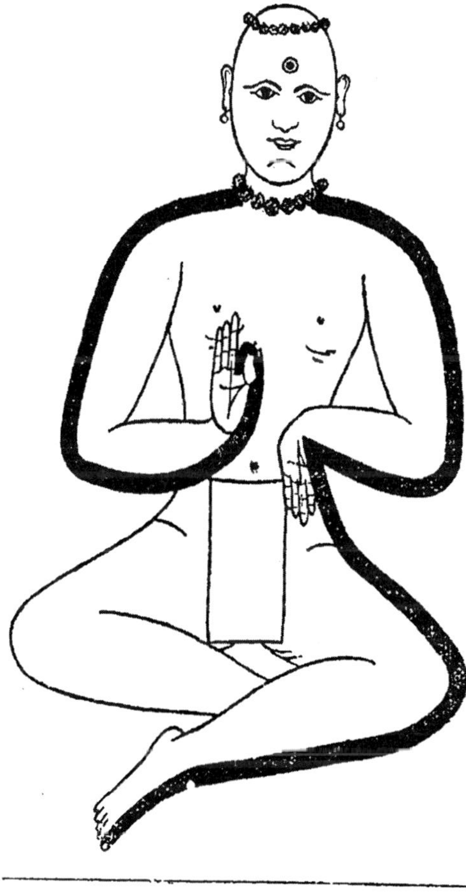